Man

of

the

Canyon

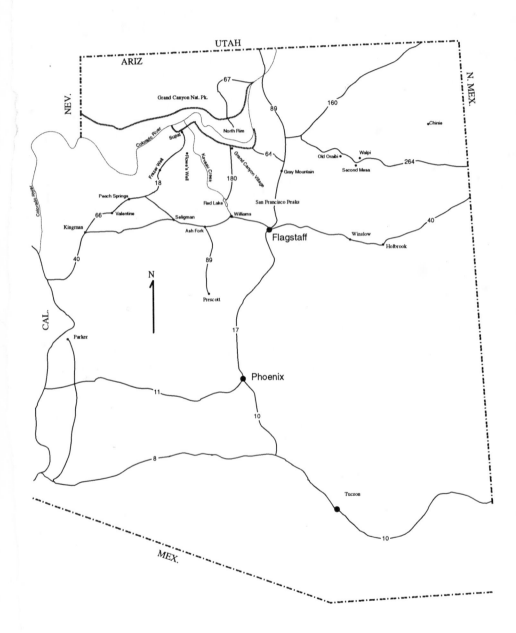

Man of the Canyon

An Old Indian Remembers His Life

As told to
Richard G. Emerick

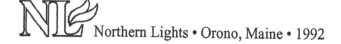
Northern Lights • Orono, Maine • 1992

Man of the Canyon

Copyright © 1992 by Northern Lights

ISBN 1-880811-06-5 (cloth)

ISBN 1-880811-07-3 (paper)

Library of Congress Catalog Number: 92-062434

For Marilyn

CONTENTS

Introduction

I picked up a lot of pinkish Supai sand in my sneakers walking along the trail toward Mark Hanna's house on that warm, spicy-smelling morning. The sand was fine-grained and soft but had built up uncomfortably in my shoes. I sat down on a rock beside the creek to empty them.

Here I was back in the canyon again. Many years before, when I was only a boy, I had seen the Grand Canyon for the first time. To stand at the edge of such immense beauty nearly silences the heart. It had been that way when I first saw it. It was that way still. It is one of the few places where one may experience the hope that the determined efforts of our species to destroy this beautiful earth may at last be overwhelmed by nature. In the presence of such eternal splendor any sensitive and perceptive person must recognize and acknowledge our fleeting insignificance.

To descend into the canyon from the rim is an experience beyond almost any other. Before beginning the descent, one looks across to the other side so far beyond the reach of all the senses except sight and even that is dimmed by the vastness of space that must be measured in thousands of feet and even miles. I remember the first time thinking, "Am I really going down there into that gigantic maw? Is it possible there is a way into it that ancient people found? What kind of people could they have been and what kind of people are their descendents?" I should have understood that such ancient people living and wandering in the southwest were accustomed to living with hugeness and vastness so that even this great canyon country would leave them undaunted.

The very first step on the trail from the rim into the canyon is a step over a precipice. There is nothing gradual in a descent down the face of a cliff. The trail, traveled by these people and their sturdy, patient horses for hundreds of years, makes its way through jumbled blocks of stone the size of buildings. These have been calved by the sheer faces of cliffs that rise thousands of feet above as the journey down continues. The warm fragrance of the scrubby vegetation wells up in one's face along with the dry hotness of the canyon breezes. The plaintive sobbing song of the canyon wren is everywhere. Every sound of voice, footstep and hoof echoes from the great walls. Then, after all those miles of travel in a three thousand foot descent, the trail straightens, levels, and finally opens into an Eden-like place through which a gentle blue-green stream called Havasu Creek flows. It is Cataract Canyon and it is so lush and green as to take one's breath away. The sound of peoples' voices and the play of children seems almost alien in this loveliness, but it is their home. The home of the Havasupai people. It has been so for hundreds of years.

The Havasupais have occupied this canyon and a vast region on the plateau for at least 600 years with little or no competition from any other groups. By occupancy, however, is not implied any concentration of population. Into this area occasionally wandered small family groups or hunting expeditions. There is little indication that they ever engaged in warfare in defense of this area and undoubtedly were little disturbed by other hunters contacted in the region. The post-contact years saw their original homeland extensively and illegally eroded. However, in January 1975, after long legal battles, President Gerald Ford signed PL 93-620 which restored 251,000 acres of their traditional lands.

The area most consistently occupied today is that of the village located in Cataract Canyon. Here about seven miles above its confluence with Grand Canyon, Cataract Canyon broadens to about one quarter mile in width for a distance of over a mile. The cultivation of perhaps one hundred and twenty acres of this bottom land is made possible by Havasu (Cataract) Creek which rises from the Canyon floor about a mile above the village and, increasing in volume, flows over a series of spectacular waterfalls to join the Colorado River in Grand Canyon. The village itself is farther upstream than it was in earlier days.

The presence of water in this part of the canyon has sharply set it off from the surrounding country for it is richly green with willows, cottonwoods, mesquite and orchards of peach and fig trees. Pear, apricot, pecan, pomegranate and apple trees are scattered here and there throughout the irrigated fields. Most of these fruits were acquired from contact with early Mormon settlers to the North and West. The talus slopes which lie at the foot of the red sandstone walls forming the canyon are covered with a variety of low bushes. The bench area above the walls is sparsely covered with yucca and scrubby mescal. This intermediate plateau spreads out on both sides of the canyon to the foot of the "white wall" which rises vertically to the plateau above, which is dotted with sagebrush until it sweeps to a higher elevation near Grand Canyon station where juniper, cedar, piñon and even ponderosa pines grow in abundance.

The annual precipitation both on the plateau and in the canyon, varies from five to eighteen inches and is nearly confined to two periods. The heaviest rains, which are sudden and torrential, fall in the summer months, usually between the beginning of June and the end of September. The runoff from the plateau areas during these storms often accumulates into small flood crests which sweep through the canyons as they push toward the Colorado River. Such floods have frequently caused damage to the village in Cataract Canyon and nearly always render the irrigation system useless until it is repaired. The snowfall is usually heavy on the plateau, but seldom covers the canyon floor to a depth of more than a few inches at any one time.

The plateau is some three thousand feet above the village in Cataract Canyon and the temperatures are consistently lower by about ten degrees throughout the year. Since the plateau offered a better supply of wood, however, some of the Havasupais were able to keep warmer by moving there during the cold months. More important, however, was the fact that the hunting and gathering aspect of their food-getting economy was carried out at this time. The women harvested wild seeds and the men hunted deer and antelope. Some of the trading with other tribes was carried out during this part of the year also.

Formerly, the Havasupais held farmlands at Indian Gardens on the Bright Angel trail below Grand Canyon station and possibly other places in their territory such as Prospect Valley or the area around the San Francisco Peaks. All agricultural pursuits today, however, are carried out in Cataract Canyon.

The Havasupai village area in the canyon consists of five hundred and eighteen acres and is divided into more than one

hundred and eighty distinct plots of land. Often several continu-
ous plots are owned by the same individual, yet they are fenced
off from each other or in some way set apart.

Throughout the literature on Supai, especially that of a
more popular nature, the isolation of this village is always
emphasized. While it is true that some three thousand feet of
rock walls surround it, there certainly is little barrier to traffic
today nor was travel in and out of the canyon ever much of a
problem to the Havasupais in the past. Passing in and out of the
canyon is no lark, to be sure, but neither is it the gruelling
experience as which it has at times been portrayed.

Foot trails were always sufficicient, though dynamite, picks,
and shovels have certainly improved several of the horse trails
since pre-historic times. At present there are seven horse trails
and three others which can only be followed on foot. The horse
trails range in length from eight to fifty miles and approach the
canyon from three directions. The foot trails are all fairly short,
the longest being only three and a half miles long. All of them,
however, begin from points on the plateau which are extremely
difficult to get to by car.

Supai, then, is accessible from nearly all sides and there is
every evidence that it has been so for a very long time. The foot
trails are not always obviously marked but for those who know
the country they are easy enough to follow, making it possible to
reach the plateau at a number of points from the village.

The plateau area between the top of the inner gorge (red
wall) and the bottom of the outer gorge (white wall) is also
marked by trails, for it has long afforded a place to graze horses
and gather mescal. This flat expanse of grubby vegetation has a
few intermittent springs where stock may drink, except in particularly dry seasons. Abandoned shelters and camps can be
seen and some are still used by those who pasture their horses
there.

The Havasupais speak a dialect which, along with the Hualapais, the Tonto and the Yavapais has been classified as the eastern division of the Yuman stock. Havasupai and Hualapai are particularly close, the dialects being no more different form each other than "Bostonian" and "Brooklynese". The cultural affinities of these two groups are equally close and their members live comfortably in each others midst and inter-marriage is common. Relations with the Hopis in the past have been very close. The Hopis have even introduced traits which are uncommon in the cultural pattern of the Yuman speaking people. The Havasupais and Hualapais have frequent disagreements on individual, family and tribal levels, but the linguistic, cultural, and geographical closeness of the last two groups has always kept them closely bound together.

Other than the Hualapais, the Havasupais historically, had contact with the Navajos, Hopis, Mohaves, Zunis, Yavapais, Piutes, White Mountain and Tonto Apaches and perhaps others. First recorded white contact was in 1776 with the party of the Spanish missionary Padre Francisco Garces, which was guided to Cataract Canyon by Hualapais.

Havasu Creek. What a beautiful little stream it is. Exactly blue-green in color, it has made life possible in the canyon for the Havasupai Indians for hundreds of years. I sat for a few minutes and wondered at my being there. When I first came to this canyon in 1949 as an anthropology student I decided then to make these people in this place the subject of a field study. In 1950, when I was accepted into the Ph.D. program in anthropology at the University of Pennsylvania I was determined to make an ethnographic survey of these people the subject of a thesis. Service in the U.S. Marine Corps during the Korean War intervened, but by 1953 I had already made three field trips to the canyon to carry out the study and had more than enough material to write a thesis. Still, I was dissatisfied. I knew about kinship, land tenure, family and political structure, material culture, etc. but I knew that was not enough. I needed to get a feeling for what it was like to be a person living in this time, in this place and in this culture. It was not enough to see the structure of Supai life. I wanted to feel its texture as well. It is in the lives of individuals that this dimension can be felt. Most ethnological monographs do not give the reader and other scholars that feeling. I did not want to make that kind of methodological error.

I had come to know a number of the people who lived in the canyon quite well and a few of them I felt I could call friends. I asked some of these people who would be a good informant for the kind of life history material I wanted. Two of my advisors suggested Mark Hanna and I agreed with them. He was seventy-one years old and had a long and often exciting life behind him. He had frequently lived for periods of time in out-of-canyon places as a cowboy, a hunter and trapper and even as a showman. He was generally well respected by the Supais and by the neighboring Hualapai People as well and he had many friends and connections among the Hopi People in the pueblos to the east. His life time had already spanned a period of very profound changes in Havasupai history. Mark was, in fact, looked upon with a certain amount of awe by many of his fellow tribesmen.

Ash Canyon is a little 2-3 acre side canyon emerging from the east flank of Havasu Canyon. This is where Mark Hanna and his sister Susie, nearly twenty years older than he, lived on their land. As I approached the house, notebook in hand and a pocket full of pencils, there was no one about, but I was pleased to see two chairs set carefully in the shade of a very large cottonwood which grew about fifty feet or so from the house. I was pretty sure that the outdoor setting would be where I would conduct my interviews with Mark. The Supais, I had noticed, did not often invite visitors into their houses and usually sat or stood around outside to chat rather than intrude into the busy work which goes on inside the houses or hogans.

Back in the early 1950s many of the Havasupais still lived in hogans, which are pole and brush and earthen structures, usually conical in shape. However, a number of families lived in small, simple wooden houses most of which had been brought into the canyon by government mule trains as a relief measure following the disastrous flood of 1911 that wiped out the entire village. Mark and Susie lived in one of these.

I had seen Mark fairly often during my visits to the village. He knew who I was and why I was there but we had never spoken directly to each other beyond my saying hello as we passed on a trail. On such occasions he was usually on a horse and I was walking. After I spoke to him he would courteously nod his head but never smile or speak. He was a somewhat formidable individual who was not either friendly or unfriendly. He had an immense and quiet dignity beyond any other Supai I had met. He was, though in his early seventies, a lean, wiry, energetic man, about 5'1" tall who appeared to be in robust health and who, when he sat his horse with the straight-backed confidence born of a lifetime of having done so, appeared to add greatly to his stature.

Because so many of the Havasupais spoke some English I had, unfortunately, not learned much of their language. Mark spoke English quite well which was yet another reason for interviewing him. He had, in fact, been an interpreter for the anthropologist Leslie Spier in 1918. Actually, I was to find that the way he used the language was itself a colorful and almost artistic dimension of his narrative and often revealed subtleties of personality and experience that would otherwise have been missed. I had no recording device and knew I would have to employ a kind of speed writing. I hoped to be able to take down what he spoke as nearly verbatim as possible. As it turned out I was able to do so. Mark simply related the events at his own speed and in his own manner with as few interruptions from me as possible. Thus the events spoken of were those which he thought were important and relevant to the story of his life. It was obvious that he was rather proud of the "adventures" in his life and especially of the many jobs which he has had on the "outside." He was always ready to talk about them, often to the exclusion of details between such episodes. Since, on occasion, he became slightly but noticeably annoyed when such gaps in the story were pointed out to him, I thought it advisable not to press him too hard for the intermediate material. I was also loathe to interrupt the flow of the narrative more than necessary to keep up with him. If I asked him to stop for a moment so that I could catch up with him, it didn't seem to break his continuity of thought. If I asked him a question or requested a few more details it often broke that continuity.

Throughout the course of the interviews, Mark was conscious of maintaining the correct sequence of events although the first dozen years were somewhat confused in this respect and he was inclined to jump around, regardless of the chronology, and to remember only certain events and little of what happened to connect them. He frequently described his childhood as being, "just like dreaming." In recounting these early years Mark displayed a good recollection of the childhood point-of-view.

At no time did Mark's perseverance falter. He always appeared to be most willing to begin each interview and never was the one to suggest that it be terminated. The length of the session varied little and usually consumed not more than two and one-half hours. Often as much as one-fourth of this time was spent discussing some village gossip or what Mark planned to do with this or that horse, or what cottonwoods he intended to trim for fence posts or firewood or which field would be planted in alfalfa next year. Sometimes Mark asked me to relate certain episodes in my own life. I frequently used this settling down period before each interview as an opportunity to cross-check with Mark on some data which I had collected from other informants. Then, after both Mark and I had our roots well planted into the morning the more formal aspect of the interview would begin. I always read back to him the last hundred words or so from the previous day and he would take up the narrative from there.

Whenever possible Mark's account of an event to which other Supais were also witnesses was cross-checked. For example the effects of the 1911 flood as described by Mark closely correlates with that given by several other men and women, none of whom were with him at the time. Theodore Roosevelt's visit to Grand Canyon was witnessed by a number of Supais still living and here again Mark's account, though certainly not detailed, is given credence by several others, thus engendering confidence both in Mark's honesty and his memory. Still this is not to say that such comparison of data always served to bear out precisely what Mark narrated, but the number of notable discrepancies was small and often merely the result of a difference in viewpoint. Mark knew that I was cross-checking on his data, but never seemed to object.

There, in Ash Canyon, on a fine June morning in 1953 it was all to begin. I had the feeling that I was about to embark on an exciting adventure. To be allowed inside another person's life and world was a matter of great anticipation and humbling honor. When Mark's door opened and he stepped out to greet me and shake my hand I felt that in taking the first step with him down the road of his life, my own life was about to take a turn as well.

Richard G. Emerick

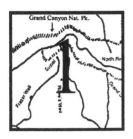

Remembering, Dreaming

In the Spring, seventy-one years ago, I was born. I think it was at the last part of March. My mother was called Tokaoridja and she was up at Drift Fence out of the canyon picking piñon nuts. My real father died right after I was born and my mother was with another man. His name was Hanna and me and my brother and sister, we called ourselves Hanna for a last name because he was our stepfather and he treated us like we were his real children. My mother was half Hualapai, but my real father was Supai.

Sometimes I think I remember things from when I was just a baby but maybe somebody told me these things and it's like I remember them. I don't know if little babies remember. Sometimes I think I remember things and maybe I dreamed them and they seem like remembering. I think I remember when I was still a little baby in the cradleboard my mother tied a little bag of corn to my chest to make my chest flat and wide. All the time I was in that cradleboard my mother kept that on me. That thing

1

was called *Wy-jee-wóy-a*. It means "heart." They don't put those on babies anymore. My sister, Susie, told me I was in a cradleboard for a long time. She said it had a mattress made from cedar bark on it and there was rabbit skin over the bark. Susie said she carried me like I was her baby sometimes. Susie never had her own babies.

Sometimes when I was little I pissed in my bed and I didn't know where the water came from. Sometimes I thought it was rain. The blankets got all wet. Those blankets were made from cedar bark and rabbits skin and when they got wet with piss I remember they would stink. It scared me when I didn't know where the water came from. I didn't feel it when I pissed it and I didn't know I did it. It scared me and I cried. My mother spanked me when she found those blankets wet. Maybe she thought I did it because I wanted to. I don't think babies do things because they want to get spanked but people spank them like they did those things to be bad. I don't think they do.

Right after I was born my mother put holes in my ears. She made the holes with a needle and then she put sticks in them to keep those holes open. I don't have those holes no more. They all closed up a long time ago. I don't know if I ever wore things in those holes. I don't remember that.

When I was little I got scared easy. Sometimes somebody would just put his hand in front of me and it scared me and then I cried. It was easy for me to cry when I was little. Susie says I cried lots of times when I was little. I don't remember why I did that.

When I was a little boy I hollered to the walls in the canyon and I heard the hollering when it came back. I did it one day when I was little and it was like somebody else hollering to me. Maybe I thought I had somebody to play with out there. I liked it a lot so I hollered all the time. I did it so much my mother spanked me sometimes. After that I always got scared when I

heard hollering or somebody shoot a gun and it came back from
the walls. It scared me and my mother told me I should always
run when I hear noises like that. She said, "You run and you
find me when you hear anybody hollering or if you hear guns
shooting." I always did that.

When I was a little boy I was just dreaming. I didn't know
my real father. I never saw who he was. He was married with
another woman before he was my mother's husband and that
woman had a boy baby and his name was Chickapaniga. My
real father was his father and we are brothers. My mother used
to say to me when I was little, "Your real father died right there",
and she pointed to a place. That was up at Drift Fence. I think I
could see him sometimes when she said that. They burned him
up there when he died. My mother was married with Hanna
when I was still little. Hanna was good to me and my brother
and Susie. When I was old enough to learn to swim Hanna
showed me how to swim. He told me to keep out of the deep
water and he said when I get cold in the water, I should come out
of the water and get in the warm sand. He said, "Don't kick sand
in other fellows eyes when you're in the sand." My mother told
me when we have a flood and all the water in the stream is
muddy, not to swim in that muddy water because it is heavy then
and maybe I'll drown if I swim in it. I would have swam in the
water when it was muddy if she didn't tell me not to do it.

My clothes were rabbit skin and they kept me plenty warm
in the winter. In the summer when I was little I didn't wear any
clothes sometimes. My mother picked seeds and corn and some
kinds of weeds too. I don't know what the name of all of them
was but that's what we ate. We had to eat mescal then too. My
mother found it and roasted it and that's what we ate. We didn't
have no groceries then in those old times. We had rabbits and
squirrels and antelope and sheep once in a while. Sometimes we
didn't have enough to eat where we lived and I got hungry when

I played and I cried if I didn't have nothing to eat. Then sometimes I climbed up on the cliff over there to that cave where my old Uncle Smiley lived. He gave me food sometimes. He gave it to my sister, Susie, and my brother too.

My mother worked all the time in her garden and picked weeds and seeds and stuff and sometimes she didn't have no time to cook food. So sometimes we were hungry. We even ate soapweed if we were out of food. My mother always worked all the time to get food for us.

Hanna made a bow and arrow for me when I was little and he showed me how to shoot that bow and arrow and he showed me how to make one too and how to put feathers on it. He didn't put no points on those arrows because it might scare me if I saw those points and I might hit somebody. I never had points on my arrows. They just scared me, that's all. Sometimes when we played with other boys they broke our arrows and we broke theirs too. Some of those boys were mean. My mother told us not to be mean. She said, "People don't like mean boys." I know they don't like mean men too.

Sometimes I would steal melons and corn from people's gardens. She told me, "You keep away from that fellow's land." She would spank me, but I told her, "you don't have enough food for me so I'll go steal it from some other fellow." Then she'd hit me but I stole stuff the next day anyways, sometimes. My mother always worked to get us food but sometimes it wasn't enough.

My mother told me not to fight with other boys, so I and my brother never learned to fight. I don't know how to hit with my hands now even and my brother, Henry, doesn't either. We stayed away from mean boys. One time some boys took my arrows when I was little and I chased them and threw rocks at them to scare them good but I didn't hit them. A boy threw a rock at me and hit my head and it bled. Another boy hit me in the mouth with a rock and made this mark here and another boy shot an arrow at my brother and hit him near his eye, but my mother and my uncle told us not to fight so we didn't fight them back. Hanna never told us not to fight but he didn't fight himself. I heard when he was a boy he was fighting a lot though. I never fought with my brother or my sister. I never fought with a girl. My mother didn't remember much about fighting with the Apache and the Yavapai, but her brother, my Uncle Smiley who lived in the cave, said he and my mother used to run and hide in the rocks when the Apaches and the Yavapais used to come down here to fight. They told us it is better to run than to be fighting.

When I was a little boy I didn't know nothing but my mother told me things. My mother made me be good and she didn't let me go out of this here canyon and get in trouble. My mother told me to get up early before the sun and run and run. My mother said I should do this and then when I'm older I'm used to getting up early and I'll keep getting up early so I can see rabbits and other things to hunt for. Lots of boys used to run that way every morning. When I was little, most of the people lived down below where the village is now so I would wait up here by Ash Canyon till a bunch of boys ran by and then I ran out and caught up with them and we all ran together. Some of those boys carried some fire with them, but I never did. I wore a little sheep bell so people would know I am running. Some of those other boys wore bells too and we all hollered when we ran and people watched us when we went by. Most of those boys just wore a shirt when they ran and that's all I wore too. Lots of times when we finished running we all jumped in the stream. Even in the winter we did this. All the time I was a boy I ran like this every morning. I quit when I'm still a boy. When I went to school, I quit.

When I was a little boy I used to dream that I would be climbing on the cliffs and fall or that I was swimming and I began to drown. When I woke up from having those dreams I was scared and I cried. It was a real thing to me. I used to dream that I was on a horse and the horse would shake the bridle off and run away with me, and I would hang on and hang on and then fall off. Sometimes I dreamed the horse would climb right up the cliffs with me on him and when we got way up I would fall off and fall down to the bottom of the cliff. When I grew up and I learned how to ride good, I didn't dream that anymore. When I dreamed it was real to me and I was scared.

The Hopis, Our Friends—The Ghost Dance Comes

All the Supais have horses. We always had them and every Supai man wants as many horses as he can get and take care of. Some men have more than they can take care of so they sometimes just wander off in the canyons or go up on top. We use horses sometimes to trade for things and to give people and sometimes we eat them if they are too old or sick or broken up or if we are too hungry for some meat.

Mostly we have horses because it is too hard to go places and get out of the canyon if we have to walk. This country is a hard place to get to places in if we don't have horses. We always had them. Sometimes women have horses. I always had horses. I will have horses always.

The first time I rode a horse for a long way was one time we went to Oraibi to trade with the Hopis. Lots of women roasted mescal and made baskets to take to the Hopi to trade for blankets and corn and stuff. My mother told me, "We are going to the Hopis and we call those people brothers." I rode all the way on top of a load of mescal that my mother was taking to trade for blankets. It cut my legs on that rough mescal and they were all sore when we got to Oraibi. It took four or five days to get there. We mostly used to go once a year when it was spring and the days were good. In the winter it was too cold to go and in the summer it was too hot. I liked to go to the Hopis when I was little. I like those people and they call me a friend. I still go there if I can.

The first time we went to the Hopis I went with my brother and my mother and my old uncle and Hanna. The first night we camped on Grey Mountain. That's near the place they call Desert View now in the park. It was cold and some snow came down. Hanna and my uncle made a little brush house and we stayed inside. All day long I was digging my head with a stick. When I started to go to sleep my mother looked in my hair and she found bugs so she sharpened a knife and cut it. My hair was long down to my shoulders and, Jesus Christ, it hurt when she cut it and I cried and hollered and my mother slapped my face and hit my body. When my hair was cut short, she brushed out those bugs. It took a long time. My mother said I was sleeping too much and that's why I got bugs. She told me I should get up more early and run more before the sun comes up and rub my head hard and then I won't have bugs. Most of the boys had long hair in those days, but some of them cut it all but a little bunch on top of their heads. They said it was to put feathers on. I never had my hair that way, but some boys did and some of the men too. My Uncle Smiley said he had his hair that way once. All the boys and men have their hair cut short now. They don't want white people to say, "Look at those Indians."

We stayed in that shelter on Grey Mountain a few days till the snow stopped coming and then we went to Oraibi. The snow was deep then and the horses had some hard times. Lots of Supais went that year. We didn't have much food and we stayed at the house of a friend of Hanna's. We stayed inside his house all winter and they gave us corn to eat and we didn't give them nothing for it. Their house was warm in the winter and the women did a lot of things like working skins and cooking lots of food and make designs on things. The men talked and laughed a lot of times and the kids played and chased rabbits and I learned to talk Hopi pretty good. They fed us just like relatives. The Hopis are good people, but the Navajos aren't much. We don't like Navajos much. They seem like strange people. Not like Indians. They talk funny and they lie and steal and even kill other Indians sometimes.

When we came back down here, when it was spring, those Hopis gave us corn to bring back down here with us, so we would have some to plant because we had eaten all our own corn up in the year before. We grew lots of good corn in that summer and the next time we went to Oraibi we took some of that corn to the Hopis to pay them back. My mother and the other women, they made baskets to take too and we took some of that red dirt we have around here and mescal and salt from the cave down on the Colorado River. Sometimes the Hopis didn't have enough food so they came down here and we fed them like they fed us. Sometimes they stayed a long time but we always got along good. My mother told me about lots of times when the Hopis came down here and we fed them. We took care of each other. We don't talk the same language but we learn each other's language. It's not hard to do. Nobody can learn Navajo language.

Not very long after we got back from Oraibi my old uncle got sick and a Hualapai doctor came down here and he brought his brother too. That Hualapai was called Doctor Tommy and he was a real little man with a lump on his back. They had a sing for my uncle and that was the first time I went to a sing. They sang for my uncle for four nights and they sang all night every time. It was cold at night and my mother wrapped me up in a rabbit skin blanket. I was glad I went to that sing and I thought maybe I would like to sing like that sometime. I asked my mother, "Will they cure my uncle?" She said, "Yes, they are good doctors and they can cure him easy." That's why I was sure they would. They cured him all right. He had coughing and sweat but he got better.

While I was still little, one time I saw Alva Jones's wife get born. I was real little but I heard her mother hollering and I went and looked and it scared me. Her hollering scared me and I saw a lot of blood too. Her hole got so big and stretched and the baby came out through the hair. My mother helped her. My mother helped lots of women like that. She knew what to do. After the baby came, she wrapped it up and then the next morning she told the woman to get up and run and carry some fire in a roll of cedar bark and burn herself on the inside and outside of her knees and ankles so she won't get rheumatism. That was the first time I ever saw a baby get born. I don't like to see that.

Not long after that there was an old woman who was a widow who died. They called her Jane. When I heard an old woman died, I asked my mother who she was and she wouldn't tell me. She said, "When a man or woman dies no one should say the name for a long time, maybe three or five years. She said it could call back the ghost and make trouble. The relatives of that woman put all her clothes on her and took her on a horse down near Havasu Falls where there was a lot of wood laying around and they burned her up. I went down there and I watched when they burned her. I was close so I could hear her burn up. I was scared for the ghosts because my mother told me about them. Those relatives tore down that woman's house and broke her pottery and burned it all up too. This was the first time my mother told me about ghosts. She told me to keep away from where people died because maybe the ghosts would kill me. I never saw no ghosts when I was little. I was just dreaming that's all. My mother told me about ghosts, but she said she never saw none. She believed there were ghosts and she said maybe she'd see one some day. I don't know if she ever did.

One time when I was still little, I was with some other boys and Chief Manakadja came over where we were and he told us that one time all kinds of Indians lived together up in the place where the Hualapais live. All those Indians lived together. He said there were so many Indians they couldn't be counted. Some of them were Hopi, some Apache, Piute, and Navajo. One day some of the children started fighting and after a while all of the children were fighting, so some of the women began to fight too. Then all of the women were fighting and all of the men too. All of those Indians were fighting with each other so they all split up and went all over. The Supais come down here in this canyon and lived up on the red wall where the ruins are now. Those ruins were houses they built to live in. After a while the people came down here and lived. The houses fell down. That's what he told us. I knew it was true because he was a chief and he told us.

Near that same time we heard that the government made some kind of papers and they took lots of Supai land away. Lots of people were mad about this. Captain Navajo was chief then and he saw some of those white men and made a mark on the papers saying it was all right for them to do that. People said Captain Navajo wasn't a chief no more and they were mad at him about it. They took lots of land that the Supais always lived on in the canyon and up on the top. They lived there since the beginning of the Supais.

The first time I heard people dancing and singing up farther in the canyon, I asked my mother what the noise was for and she said, "Some people are dancing." I asked her what those people were dancing for and she said they were doing it for fun. I wanted to go up there and see that dancing but she said she didn't want me to go up there. After two days they were still dancing and my mother took me and my brother and sister up there to see it. Those people were dancing a circle dance. They had a drum but nobody used a rattle. I just sat there and watched and my brother watched too, but my mother and Susie danced with those people. That was the first time I ever saw a dance. The next year there was a dance too, and I asked my mother if I could go up there alone to see it but she told me not to go because I'm still too small. Once, when I was still little, I saw a circle dance that some Supais did around a pole stuck in the ground. There was feathers on top of the pole and those people danced around it in a circle dance and sang a Hualapai song Watahomigie learned from those Indians. Some of the men climbed up the pole and slid down.[1]

---

[1] In 1870 silver-bearing ore was discovered along Havasupai Creek. In 1875 silver and lead mining began below Mooney Falls on the creek. On June 8, 1880 President Rutherford Hayes issued an executive order establishing a reservation 12 miles long and 2 miles on each side of Havasupai Creek as a reservation for the Supai. This included only the farms in the canyon and specifically excluded the mining area.

On March 1931, 1882 President Chester Arthur issued an executive order making all of the traditional winter range land on the plateau public property. This he did on advice from the engineering office, Department of Arizona.

These actions made the Havasupai prime candidates for the nativistic message of the Ghost Dance movement of the Paiute Messiah, Wovoka. By the 1890s they were a part of that movement. They, in fact, continued the Ghost Dance into the first decade of the 20th Century. The Ghost Dance held in the canyon in 1895 was probably the one Mark witnessed.

White Men in the Canyon

I n the winter, we mostly went up to Mohawk Canyon, north of Frazer Well. My old uncle had grazing land up near that place. He built a house like a Navajo hogan up there on his land. My stepfather, Hanna, and my uncle had to fix the hogan every time we went up there to live in the winter. My mother got cedar bark to put on the house and my stepfather and my uncle put it on. I was too little to help and me and my brother, Henry, just played around. We didn't have things to play with, just bows and arrows. We played that we hunted with them. When it got cold and there was lots of snow we had some shoes made from rabbit skin or wildcat skin. The hair was inside and they were warm. My mother made socks for us from cedar bark. She made the cedar bark soft by rubbing it between her hands. Sometimes she mixed it with rabbit fur. When we moved from one place to another, I never knew when we were going some-place or where we were going. I didn't know nothing when I was little. It was just like dreaming.

One time when we were up near Coyote Canyon when I was still little, my uncle gave me two turquoise earrings for my ears. My uncle told me, "When you've got holes in your ears you can hear when somebody tells you to do something. Then you won't be lazy. If you don't have holes in your ears you won't hear things and maybe you'll be lazy then." My uncle made the holes in my ears and, Jesus Christ, it hurt but not for long. I had those earrings about four years and I sure was glad I had them and lots of boys wanted me to give them to them, but I kept them. I lost them one time and I never had any more. When I told my mother I lost those earrings, I thought she was going to hit me, but she didn't.

The hardest my mother ever hit me was once when we were coming back from Oraibi where we traded with the Hopis. I was near thirteen I think. Me and my brother, Henry, found a big log on the ground where we were camping and we wanted to play it was a horse, so I took a saddle blanket and we put it on that log and played it was a horse. It was cold and we built a fire there to keep warm. When we didn't want to play there any-more, we just left the fire and the blanket on the log. My mother found that blanket and it was nearly all burned from the fire. She came back to camp and she said, "What did you take that saddle blanket for? It was the only saddle blanket we had. Now it's all burned up. I'm going to beat you hard for doing this!" She picked up a stick and hit me all over my head and my body. I hollered and cried and she kept hitting me. When my brother, Henry, heard me hollering he ran away. Hanna told my mother, "What are you hitting that boy for? He's only a boy and he didn't learn not to do these things yet. You shouldn't hit him like that." My mother said, "I'll make him learn now and he won't do this again." Hanna said, "You shouldn't hit him."

My brother, Henry, stayed away all day and hid. When he came back my mother didn't hit him. She wasn't mad no more.

When it was night I heard my mother and Hanna talk about it. I don't know what they said. They just talked about it, but they didn't talk loud.

The next day my mother put some red paint and grease on my back where it was sore where she hit me. It made my back hurt worse and I cried. My mother took my hair and shook my head, "You learn now, don't you? If you do that thing again I'll hit you again. If you don't do it again it will be all right." I was sore at her, but I didn't say anything. I think if I said something she would hit me some more.

One day, when it was early in summer, I got a bad nose-bleed. My mother said, "You eat too many green peaches." The blood came out of my nose for a long time so my mother climbed up on the rocks and got some kind of weeds. I don't know what that was but she got it and she boiled some in water. It was sour. She put some of that stuff on my head and wrapped it up in some stuff. It was buckskin, I think. She said that would make me stop bleeding and it did. She told me not to eat more green peaches and I didn't eat them, but I went swimming too much in cold water and it made my body sore and I had cracks in my skin all over. My mother chewed some deer fat and spit it in some red paint and mixed it up. She greased me all over with that stuff and put it even in my eyes. It made me feel good. I told my mother, "I won't go in the cold water again." I went in before she said it was all right and my brother saw me. I told him, "Don't tell my mother. Don't tell! Don't tell!" He told her anyway and my mother hit me hard for doing that. I was sore at my brother Henry when he told my mother, but I didn't hit him. I said, "You shouldn't tell her things."

My mother never hit me after that. She only said words to me. My uncle and Hanna never hit me. Only my mother. I wasn't sore at her because she did it. I knew she did that to keep me from doing bad things or from doing things so that other people wouldn't like me.

When I was near eight or nine years old, I saw the first white man I ever saw. When it was near noontime, one day, I heard burro bells going down through the canyon. That was the white men going down to make that mine below Havasu Falls. I heard those bells and they scared me so I ran home. My mother said, "Those are white men with those burros. You keep away from those fellows."

The next day I went down with some boys to see the white men. I didn't tell my mother I'm going down there because she would say, "No," to me. When we were down there, we saw those white men and they gave us molasses and bread and coffee and sugar. They gave me some coffee to drink. I thought that stuff was too sweet and I didn't like it, but I drank it. Those men laughed when I got sick and after I threw up I laughed too and then they gave me some bread with butter on it. I didn't know what that butter was, so I scraped if off the bread before I ate it. That was the first time I ever ate bread like that. I liked it a lot. I didn't like the butter then, but I sure like it now.

After I ate all that stuff those white men gave me, I went home and I was sick all the time I was going there. When I got there I was still throwing up. My mother saw me doing that and she said, "Why are you sick?" I told her, "I went down to see the white men and they gave me bread and coffee and lots of stuff." She said, "I told you to keep away from those fellows. They'll put you in a sack and carry you away with them if you go down there again." She talked to me a lot like that, but after two or three days I went down to that place again but, I didn't tell my mother. I ate more bread and molasses, but I didn't eat butter or coffee and I didn't get sick. I didn't eat the bacon they gave me either. Those white men stayed down there quite a long time and every time some boys went down there they gave us food. We all thought they were good fellows. I watched them lots of times when they drilled hole but I didn't know what they talked about. I didn't know how they were talking. I thought their skin would be white but it was red. The next time I saw some white men after that was when we were on a trade trip at Oraibi. Those white men by Oraibi scared me more than those fellows when they came down here. When they were down here they were in my place and it didn't scare me for them to be here.

Most of the time I liked to be down there where the white men were. They didn't chase us away and I liked to see all their stuff. They had so many tools for their work and they could do lots of things the Supais didn't do. They had good clothes and hats too and big strong boots. Sometimes they let me clean some of their stuff. They were mostly clean fellows but when they worked hard some of them smelled funny. They camped by the creek and washed their clothes in the water there and their bodies too. They had lots of hair on their bodies and on their faces too.

Some of the white men asked us boys if we could get some Supai girls to come down there sometimes. They said they needed them for washing clothes. I asked some of those girls and the said that they were afraid to go down there to that camp. They said, "Those white men want girls down there to do something. They don't want clothes washed. They want girls so they can stick them."

Once one of the white men was washing his body in the creek and he told me to come in and wash his back for him. I went in there and used his chunk of soap to wash his back. He took the soap and washed my body too and he rubbed me and made my hands rub him too. I didn't know why he washed me but it kind of scared me so I ran away and I didn't go down there to those white men very much after that and I heard their burro bells when they went out of the canyon.

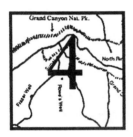

Little Boyhood Ends—
School Comes to the
Canyon—Girls and
Horses

After I was ten years old, I helped my mother in the garden. I pulled weeds and watered the corn and so did my brother and sister. I used to get hot and dirty when I did that and I used to go in the water every day to get cool and wash myself. My mother never told me to wash but I used to do it every day and I was clean when I was little.

In 1895 the school started up at the head of the water and I wanted to go but my mother told me I couldn't. She said the Hopis told her when the children start at the white men's school, they sometimes take them away and they get sickness and die. She said she wouldn't let me go. When it was the next year the teacher came here and he told my mother I had to go to that school. My mother cried and she told him she didn't want him to take me away from her and that teacher told her nobody would take none of us boys away and we could just go to school up there at the head of the water. When my mother knew that, she told him me and my brother Henry could go. We went up there on the next day. We didn't have any good clothes and the teacher gave us some to wear. I sure liked those good clothes. The teacher was a white man and his name was Mr. Bauer. He was a good man and he wasn't mean with us. He played games with us boys and he showed us how to sing songs and write letters and numbers and he even ran some races with some of the boys too. He lived right down here in the canyon and he had a wife and she had a little boy. They lived here too.

There was a lot of Supai boys at the school. I think maybe there was twenty or twenty-five. We just sat on some log seats under a tree where it was shady, and I think all those boys liked going to school. I liked it a lot. There was no girls at the school.

Mr. Bauer gave us hard bread and coffee every day and after a while I liked coffee and it didn't make me get sick. I didn't put sugar in it no more. After a while my mother thought it was good for us to go to school. She said, "You do what the teacher tells you." She said she'd hit us hard if we didn't do what Mr. Bauer told us. We had good clothes now too. We had a handkerchief and a hat and shoes.

One day my mother said, "Show me what they teach you at the school." I showed her the big letters and some numbers. I made them in the sand with my finger. My mother looked at all the things I made and told me, "When they show you what these things mean you learn it good. I don't know how long I can be here where you are. I don't know where the Indians will go or where they will live someday. If you learn all these things you can take care of yourself. You learn them good." That's what my mother said to me and she said that to my brother too and I said, "Its all right. I'll do it."

I never got in trouble at the school. The teacher never had to come and see my mother because of me or my brother, Henry. After the teacher was there for the second year, he had a big eating time for all the Indians. The government paid for it all. It was at night and my mother went to the feast and the teacher gave my mother some bread and some clothes. They gave this to all the Indians. They gave us real cups too. That was the first time we ever had real cups. Everybody used tin cans from the dump by Williams (*Wee-koo-óola* - rock riding in the middle), before we got those cups and we sure were glad to get them. They gave us buckets too and my mother threw away some of her adobe pots. Supai women didn't make pots much anymore. They got them from the Hopi. I think all the Supai pots are gone now. We all got tin and iron pots now. My mother said, "Those teacher people sure are good people and they're good to all the Indians."

When I was in the school the second year, I could read a little. In the third year the teacher showed us some figures and how to make arithmetic. My mother made a lot of baskets and sold them to some white men up on top and got some money. She saved the money and she said she was going to buy good clothes for me an my brother, Henry, up at the store at Williams. That was the only store around here anyplace. One time Little Jim went up there to that store and he didn't want to go alone so he took me with him. I was still a boy. He bought me a little flour and coffee and sugar and I gave them to my mother. When I went into that store I never was in a store before and I saw all that stuff. I saw all those clothes and the calicos and the canned stuff. I wondered where they got all that stuff and the sugar and coffee. I was thinking they made all that stuff themselves and I wondered how can anybody know how to make so much stuff. I thought the white people must have some magic to make all that stuff and those clothes.

When me and Little Jim came out of the store, I didn't ask him about what I was thinking. He didn't talk about it. The man in the store gave me some apples and some oranges because I was still a boy. When I brought those things back down here some boys asked me if I saw trees for growing those things on up at Williams. I said, "I only saw them in the store and they don't come off trees there." My mother asked me if I saw trees inside the store to grow fruits on. I told her I only saw the fruit and I don't know where it comes from. My mother asked me if I saw them make candy but I told her, "It was just there in the store and I don't know if they made it." We all wondered where they got it. My mother said, "I wonder where they get all that stuff."

When me and Little Jim were coming back from that store we stopped at a ranch halfway from Williams to here. There was a white man they called Bass that had that ranch there. He was a friend of all the Indians. He always gave them food. When we stopped there at that ranch they gave us stuff to eat and we slept in a tent with some fellows. Bass could talk our language too and his wife gave us some good clothes. She gave me some clothes her boy couldn't wear because he grew up too big for them. Those were real good clothes and I sure was glad I got them. When I came down here, my mother was glad too. Lots of those Supai boys, they asked me, "Where did you get those good clothes?" and I told them I got them at Williams and they all got the wish to go up there to that place. Some of those boys tried to get the clothes away from me, but I didn't let them. I sure liked those clothes.

When my old uncle saw me come back from Williams, he asked me if I smoked any stuff up there. I told him I didn't take anything to smoke and he said, "When you are a kid you don't smoke. It's no good when you're a kid and you smoke it's going to do something to your legs and you're going to be lazy. When you kill the coyote, then you can smoke and it's all right then, but not when you're still a kid because it will make you lazy." That's what my uncle told me.

When those white men were down here in the canyon they had stuff to smoke. They told us boys we could smoke some of their stuff if we wanted to do that. Some of us boys tried those cigarettes and they had some cigars too and a pipe. I tried to smoke one of those cigars and I coughed and got sick in my stomach. I never smoked those cigars since then but I always smoke cigarettes. It didn't make me lazy. I smoked before I killed a coyote when I could get some of those cigarettes. Us boys could sometimes take one from some of the Supai men and we would hide someplace and smoke. My mother smelled that smoke on me and she said she would tell my old Uncle. I don't think she did. He never talked about it.

After me and Little Jim came back down here from Williams, I kept on going to school. I didn't go no place else out of the canyon, I just stayed here and went to school. When the teacher asked the boys to clean up the school, everybody did it because those boys liked the teacher and we wanted to do things when he told us.

Every morning I went to get wood before school began and they used that wood to cook food at the school. Every noontime they fed us there. They gave us corned beef and rice every day and they gave us plenty. I liked that food better than what my mother gave us. She never had time to cook for us before we went to school, so I put dried peaches and dried corn in my pockets and I ate it when I'm going to school. I never said nothing to my mother about that. She said they gave us plenty of food in the school and when it was night we only had cornmeal to eat.

One day in every week we had lots of hot water by the school and we washed our clothes. Once some boys washed the lady's clothes too. Some of the boys washed her bloomers and they laughed. I never saw things like bloomers before. I told my mother about that and she said it was all right. She told me to keep away from the girls and don't try to see if they got bloomers. She said, "You're not old enough yet and it will make you lazy."

We didn't have the school in the winter. Mostly in the winter everybody goes out from the canyon. We always went to Coyote Canyon and there's plenty of wood up there. We used to come back here in the canyon in the first part of March and go to school. Some people didn't get back here for the school till maybe April. They go farther away in the winter, by Ash Fork (*Ka-theel-ka-sum-kóva* - sandstone hill) or by San Francisco Peaks. These places aren't near.

I never liked it in the winter. It was always cold and we just got wood and water for the horses and hauled water to drink and hunted for squirrels and rabbits all the winter. The hogan didn't have windows and there was only a small door. I lived in that hogan and so did my older brother Joseph, my brother Henry, my mother, Hanna, and my uncle. The fire was in the middle of the room and the smoke burned my eyes.

Every night in the winter I asked my uncle about things he can tell me. He said to me, "When I'm young, I behaved myself good. I don't go after the girls. They can give you something and your blood is poison sometimes. You behave yourself and don't go after the girls. Don't be fighting. You can break your bones just for fighting and then you'll be no good. Don't fight with people. When you're old enough, don't stay around the hogan. You'll have a bow and arrow or a gun. Don't stay home. You can hunt and you can get away and see things all around. He said the land was very big and nobody knew how far it went. He said a man should go out there on the land as far as he can and see all kinds of stuff and places. He said those other places were good to see and it helps make a man. He said to be careful about strange people out there. Wherever you go to the horses and coyotes and squirrels and deer and the other animals are all the same and you know them. The people are different in different places and you don't know them and don't know what they will do. He said the white people are more different than

Indians and he told us to watch them close and don't think you know what they will do or what they will think.

Hanna told me things like these too. He made me get up early when its morning and he told me to run and get wood. He said, "That wood is a rabbit and a deer or a squirrel and when you're older you'll be getting up early and see these things and you can hunt for them when its early." When I came in with that wood they all said, "*Haniga*—good, thank you."

Sometimes some relatives came to visit us when it was winter. Mostly they were always relatives. We never went to visit our relatives. Sometimes they came to visit us but we never did. Grand Canyon camp[2] was too far away to go there in winter and San Francisco Peaks were too far away too, so we never went to those places to visit relatives. We went to visit those Hopis more than we visited relatives.

One time a white man came to our camp in the winter when I was near fourteen. My old uncle knew how to talk in a little English and that white man talked with my uncle. He stayed at our camp three or four days and he ate our food. He asked my uncle to show him where there was lead ore in Mohawk Canyon. My uncle told him, to look at that ore he'd have to pay some money and if he wanted to dig in it he would have to pay some more money. My uncle took him to see the ore but the man never paid him money and he never came back to dig in it.

When we came back down here in the canyon I went to school and the teacher was showing us more arithmetic. One day after we were in school me and my brother, Henry, and my cousin, Fred Uqualla, we climbed up on the red wall and found some mescal when it was young and we roasted it up there and ate it. It was good like bananas and apples. We used to eat that stuff then.

---

[2] Rowe's Well

One time we found some honey in a log up there on the red wall and we brought it down here and we gave some to some other boys and to my mother. We just ate honey all day. My mother put it in water with cornmeal mush and we ate that. We sure liked it. My sister went up a few days after and she found some more honey and we had some of that too. We didn't have no groceries and jam and stuff then and the honey was good.

My mother said, "Don't go up there on those rocks and look for honey no more. There are a lot of rattlesnakes up there and you might step in them and they'll bite you and then maybe you'll die." She told me, "You go down by the falls and find lots of honey in logs." She gave me an axe to chop the logs and I found some honey there and I brought it home and we ate it.

My mother told me about a lot of sweet things to find to eat that grow around here. She told me where to find them. I learned a lot about where things grow from my mother.

One time my mother told me and my brother Henry to go up on the rocks and cut some poles. I chopped a pole and when the axe went in the wood, I heard buzzing noises all around me. There was a bees nest in the bottom of that pole. I got stung all over my head and my face and in my eyes. I ran to my brother and he picked a lot of bees out of my hair. Then I ran home. I didn't cry because I'm too old. I just laid in my bed for two days. My mother let me do that but she didn't put nothing on the stings. When I went back to school the teacher asked me if my mother put something on those stings. I said no and he put some grease all over my face and neck.

When the bees stung me I just ran and left the axe in the wood. After a few days my mother said, "You get that axe and don't leave it up there for somebody to get." I went back up there after that axe and I was scared of the bees, but I was scared more not to do what my mother said. I wrapped my head all up in cloth and just looked out through a hole. I crawled up and grabbed the axe and I ran away as fast as I could. There were still bees around that pole but they didn't sting me. When I brought back the axe my mother said, "Now, you keep away from those bees."

The teacher at the school always told the boys not to swim with the girls. There was some girls in the school too and when we went swimming in the afternoon the teacher watched the boys and the lady watched the girls. They kept us away from the girls. One time I climbed up in a tree where the girls swim. Some of the boys said the girls were in the water with no clothes on and I wanted to see that. I climbed up in that tree and I saw those girls. I saw something between their legs. Some of the boys talked about that. They said that place was where you stick them and that's where they bleed sometimes too. I already knew that and we talked about that. I thought I wanted to do that sometime but I was kind of scared. I didn't talk to girls most of the time. They seemed more different to me than strangers from another place. I wanted to see them but I didn't want to talk to them. Some boys the same age as me then were already sticking girls but I was kind of afraid then. My mother told me to keep away from the girls. I ran away from them but sometimes they caught me. One time some girls played with me by the irrigation ditch. They played with me and made it get hard and I liked it but my mother told me to keep away from those girls so I ran away.

I didn't have no horse then. My uncle let me use a horse he had. I liked to ride and I rode fast all the time. All the boys ride fast when they're boys. I didn't have no saddle. My uncle made some saddles from cottonwood and some buckskin, but he didn't let me use one. I don't think nobody had a saddle like the ones they got now. All the men made saddles. My uncle made his cinch from wool he got from the Hopis. It had a good design on it. My uncle never showed me how to make a saddle but I always watched him and I saw what he did. I never asked my uncle how to make a saddle. I didn't think I'm old enough but when I'm old enough I always knew from watching.

My mother and my uncle showed me how to make a bridle from braided soapweed and that's what I made. My mother always used a bridle like that but my uncle got a silver bridle form the Hopis and they got it from the Navajo. Maybe it was iron but it looked like silver. My uncle always used that bridle but I never used it.

One time I tied a soapweed bridle on a horse. I just learned how to make that bridle and I put it on the horse and I rode him all around. I rode fast and then the horse ran under a tree and knocked me off. I wanted to turn him, but I couldn't make him turn and the tree knocked me off when he ran under it. I got my arms and my legs hurt and I thought maybe I'll cry and I threw rocks and sticks at that horse and I chased him all over. When I went back where my uncle was, he saw bleeding on my arms and legs and he told me to tell him what happened and I told him. My uncle laughed and laughed and he told me, "Why didn't you turn that horse and don't let the tree knock you off?" I told him I couldn't turn him and he kept laughing and I wanted to throw rocks and sticks at my uncle too, but I didn't.

The next year when I was fifteen years old I still went to school all the summer. We always ate there every day and we went in the water every day too, and the teacher always watched us boys and the lady watched the girls. The teacher told us not to be around with the girls and he told us not to look between their legs if we ever saw those girls when they're swimming.

Some of the boys were talking about the girls and they said the girls bleed between their legs sometime and I wanted to know what that is so I asked my mother, "Why do they bleed there sometimes?" My mother told me, "A long time ago there weren't no tribes around here. The people who made the tribes took some sticks and broke them in pieces. They said, "This little stick is the Supais. It is a little short one but it will always be here." They pulled one hair from their head through that stick, "This short one was the Supais and the Supais aren't so big."

"A stick that was long they picked up and that was the Navajos. They pulled one long hair form their head through this long stick and said, "This long stick is the Navajos. The Navajos are tall people now."

"They took a stick that was longer than the Supai stick and shorter than the Navajo stick and they said, "This is the Hualapais." And the Hualapais are a little bigger than the Supais and not so big as the Navajos. They pulled a hair through the Hualapais stick too. That's how all those tribes were made by those people."

Then my mother told me, "When they made the Indian people they made the men and the women. When they made the men they made a little bow and arrow and then they rolled some white clay around that bow and arrow and they carried it way far in the east and laid it down there. The men and the boys were made like that. That's why boys run to the east."

My mother didn't tell me who those fellows were that made those boys and she said, "They took some white clay and they mixed it up with some blood and made it red and they took that red adobe and put it way in the west. That's why the girls run to the west and that's why girls bleed between their legs sometimes. If you go in a girl when she's bleeding there your teeth will fall out and it will be bad and maybe it will make a man a boy." My mother told me, "You keep away from girls till you're big and get some bedding and food and things and then you can go with them."

Then my uncle said to me, "If you run after girls when you're little you'll stay little and you'll have to look up to see men." That's what my mother said. That's what they told me and when I heard this I was afraid to be near girls.

Navajos, Hopis, and Fear at Williams

The year I was fifteen I didn't go to Oraibi. We didn't have no stuff to trade. Some Navajos came down here and they brought a lot of horses to trade for buckskins. They brought blankets and silver rings and belts and necklaces too. About seven of them came down here and they stayed at the place of Supai George. Supai George could talk with those Navajos and that's why they stayed there.

I never saw Navajos before and I thought they were good fellows because they danced and sang every night and some Supais danced with them. Some Supai girls danced with them and nobody said nothing about it.

My uncle gave those Navajos two buckskins and he got a mare. He told me, "You can have this horse. Take good care of him." I rode that horse around a lot and then I took him up to some pasture way up Cataract Canyon. The horse couldn't find where the water was. There was a spring there but it dried up a little. I left that horse there about a month and when I went up there to get him he was dry and thin. He was a Navajo horse and he never walked so much on rocks and not have much water. I brought him down here and he died on the next day.

I was scared to tell my uncle about that horse and I liked him because he was like a pet dog and I was sorry he died. I told my uncle right away and he said "Why didn't you take care of him good?" I told him how the horse couldn't find the water and hoofs were tender. My uncle said, "It's all right." He told me the Navajo would come back here again with another horse. I sure had a wish for another horse then and I felt sorry that horse died.

Every time the Navajo came down here there was lots of hollering and shooting in the canyon and it always made me scared and sometimes I ran away because I thought somebody was fighting.

One of the Navajos, who came down here, was called Na-eina and he was strong. James Ka-oska was married to the daughter of my old uncle and he was strong too. One time he went to where the Navajos were camped, when they were down here, and he took Na-eina's arm when he was eating and he pulled him out in the hot sand and then they wrestled just for the fun for over an hour. One of them couldn't win over the other one because they were both strong the same way. The Supais all hollered to James Ka-oska, "Squeeze him down! Make him go down!" Sometimes James would fall and sometimes the Navajo would fall but they always got up again. Every day for about four days they did that and when they went away, James Ka-oska hollered to that Navajo, "When you come back we will wrestle again." He laughed and we all laughed and everybody wanted that Navajo to come back again. I don't think he did.

After a few days some Hopis came down here and they brought a lot of blankets and some jewelry. They wanted buckskins too. The Supais had a lot of buckskins then and they hunted all over and there wasn't no rangers around here. That year I was fifteen, everybody had a lot of buckskins and nobody went out of the canyon till it was winter because lots of Indians came down here to trade for those buckskins.

The Hopis didn't dance and sing a lot or wrestle like the Navajos did, but everybody liked those Hopis better. My mother told me, "The Hopis are good people and we call them brothers. The Navajos are no good. They steal everything just like the coyotes." Those Navajos sure like the Supai girls but the girls didn't like them much and they didn't go off with them.

When the Hopis were down here they sang a ceremonial and lots of Supais went to watch. They didn't dance. They just sat still and sang with the drum. Some Supais said, "Why don't you dance?" and those Hopis said, "We're just singing." I watched them when they sang and I thought I'd like to learn that sing but it was too hard to learn. Some Supais learned it, but I didn't.

Most of the time the Hopis didn't sing, when they were down here. They just traded and went away. They always stayed with my relative, Sinyella. He could talk like a real Hopi. That's why they stayed at his place down there. Sinyella stayed at Oraibi lots of times when he was a boy. That's how he could talk that language. He stayed there every winter when he was a boy.

Hanna got a blanket for mé from the Hopis that year. He gave two buckskins for it. It was a big sized blanket to cover up with. I didn't have a horse so I couldn't hunt for buckskins yet and I never learned to shoot good when I'm young. Hanna had a long rifle '44 but I never shot a deer with it. I only shot a rabbit once with it. I didn't like that gun. It was heavy and made a lot of noise and the bullet went wherever it wanted to.

When I was seventeen I still went to the school at the head of the water. That year a different teacher came there. The other

teacher went away. The new teacher was Wilson. He came
down here with his wife and they treated us good too. They fed
us and gave us clothes and I was captain at the school then. All
those boys drilled with Indian clubs and I was captain of the
drill. I sure liked to swing those clubs and I could do it good and
that's why I was captain.

The new teacher didn't watch the boys and the girls when
they were swimming and the boys and the girls swam together in
the same place. The teacher didn't say nothing when we were
swimming together.

When it was the Fourth of July in that summer I wanted to
go to Williams. Supai Charley had a buckboard up at Hualapai
Hilltop and he was going to Williams. My sister, Susie, was
married with him and he was going to take her and his daughter
with him. I wanted to go but they didn't say I could go. My
mother didn't want me to go but I ran after them up to the head
of the water, when they were going out of the canyon up to
Hualapai Hilltop. I didn't have no shoes, but I ran all the way
up. My feet were cut and they were sore. I caught up with them
at the head of the water and I said, "I want to go." My sister was
sore at me because I didn't tell my mother and my mother didn't
want me to go. My sister said, "You can't go." and when she
said that Supai Charley said, "You shouldn't tell him that. If he
wants to go, let him go." He let me get on his horse behind him
and I rode up to Hilltop on the back of his horse.

The first night we camped at Howard Springs about half
way to Williams. My sister stopped being sore at me and she
talked to me then. The next day we went to Williams. Before
we went into where all the people are in the place, we went to the
dump where all those people throw stuff. We looked for clothes.
I found a pair of overalls, three shirts and two pairs of shoes. I
put on one of those shirts and the overalls and some shoes and I
was sure glad when I put that stuff on. I found a hat too and I put

that hat on too. I sure was glad of it. It made me feel pretty good and then we went into the town and I walked around. There was some Supai boys there too. Supai Charley bought me some marbles in the store and I played marbles with those boys. I never played marbles before and I lost all those marbles.

I watched the celebration and the bronc riding and the calf roping and horse racing. Some white boys had foot races too. There was a band from Phoenix there. I never heard a band before. There was Indians in that band too and I wished I could play in that band. I wanted to talk to those boys in the band but I just watched them. They had uniforms on. Those uniforms were like black and I wanted to touch one of them, but I just watched. They had big badges on their hats and I wondered if maybe they were policemen when they weren't in that band and I was afraid a little.

There was lots and lots of people there and they were all different kinds and it scared me a little. I never saw so many white people before and there was more white people than Indians and after a while I ran all around and I found Supai Charley and I held on to his hand and stayed with him. He didn't say nothing to me. He just held on to my hand and walked with me to a place where it was away from the noise and all those people and it was more quiet. We just stayed there and didn't say nothing for maybe it was near an hour. I didn't tell Supai Charley that I was scared to be there where there was so many people and all that noise like I was in a different world. He knew what I was feeling like. I think and he knew it was a good thing to go someplace quiet and not say nothing. He didn't let go my hand for a while and we just sat there. I thought maybe he knew what I was feeling like and I thought maybe he felt the same way. Maybe he did sometime way back when he was a boy and went to some place like Williams when there was a big, noisy time. Maybe somebody took him away from there for a while too. I was glad Supai Charley did that for me and I thought someday I'll tell him about that. I never did.

Pretty soon we went back to our camp near Howard Springs. My sister and Supai Charley's daughter bought some bread in the town and we ate it at the camp. I was glad we were away from Williams. It just scared me a lot, but I sure liked to eat that bread.

When I came back down here from Williams, I came with Supai Jack. He had some horses to drive back down here, so I came back with him and helped him drive those horses.

When I got back here my mother said, "What's the matter with you that you didn't tell me you went to Williams? I thought maybe something happened to you when you didn't come back here. I asked these boys all over where you are and not for a long time did they tell me you are at Williams. They told me and I was sorry you didn't have some money for buying food. How did you eat?" I told her Supai Charley gave me food and she said she was glad. She wasn't sore at me. I thought she'd be sore at me, but she wasn't.

The next day I went up to the schoolhouse. The teacher was sore at me because I ran off and he made me work and clean up the school and wash clothes. He made me do this because I ran off. He said if I went off someplace to get horses or go someplace, I should tell him so he can say, "It's all right." He said he would give me a licking if I didn't tell him things like that. I was kind of scared of him and I didn't run off. He said I could have a uniform if I didn't run off and I wanted that uniform a lot. I didn't get it.

My sister, Susie, wasn't really married with Supai Charley when we went to Williams, but when they came back down here, Susie went to Supai Charley's place and stayed there and then she was really married with him. That's where they lived. Sometimes they came up here and saw my mother. Susie never had any babies and I went down there where they lived lots of times and she was always glad when I came down there and Supai Charley was glad too.

My cousin, Prince Wodo, was my old uncle's son and he had some horses up near Coyote Canyon. He brought some down here. I borrowed a real saddle from my uncle and I helped Prince Wodo break those broncs. I liked to do that and I was wishing he had lots more broncs to break and I didn't get thrown off very much. Prince Wodo gave me three of those horses so I had three horses. I didn't have a good saddle but I used a saddle of Hanna's. It was a saddle made from cottonwood and buckskin and I made a bridle of soapweed.

I kept those horses in a corral and I rode them all the time. I rode a horse to the school every day. Some other boys had horses too, and we always rode horses to school.

Hanna gave me two Navajo blankets and he made some moccasins and he gave them to me too and he gave me some clothes. Now I had my own stuff. I had a lot of stuff of my own and I had some horses too. Hanna told me when he is dead all his stuff and all his horses and his garden . . . and his peach trees will belong to me and my brothers but not to Susie because she's married to Supai Charley. He said, "Don't let nobody have this stuff."

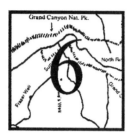

School Out of the Canyon—More Girl Trouble

When I was nineteen years old, I was still going to the school at the head of the water down here. Wilson was teacher then. In November, in that same year, it snowed down here in this canyon. Everybody said, "It isn't good." It snowed three days and then it got warm and it rained. The water in the stream was all steaming, but the water was warm. My mother told me to jump in the water and get a bath when its warm. I got in the water and it was warm but it was cold when I got out. My mother said, "When you are young don't be afraid when its cold." All the old people said that.

When it was December, school stopped at Christmas. The teacher always told us that Christmas was for Jesus when he's born in a barn. Some people loved that Jesus and they take him toys and lots of stuff and those people always do this when its Christmas. The teacher gave us candy and a handkerchief and when I was nineteen, that Christmas, I got a knife. I was sure glad of it. I liked Christmas pretty good. I always asked the teacher when it was going to be Christmas and he always told me it's December.

When we went up to Mohawk Canyon in that winter, it sure was cold. When I went out to bring in water it was all ice and I chopped up big pieces and tied them up with weeds. I tied the ice on the horse and brought it back to camp. My mother broke up that ice and put it in pots near the fire and that's where we got water for drinking.

We didn't go to the Hopis for a long time. Everybody had corn to eat and corn to plant and we didn't go to the Hopis for a long time.

When I came back down here the next year, I just went to school and rode broncos. That's all I could do. I broke some more horses for Prince Wodo. He didn't give me no more of those horses, but I broke some more.

One day my uncle said he was going to kill a horse. The horse belonged to my uncle's older brother. He lived in a cave near that one my uncle lived in. They had two fellows help them and those two fellows held that horse by two ropes on the horse's neck. My uncle shot him behind his front leg with an arrow and then he ran up and pulled the arrow out. That horse stood still for a while and then he jumped around and those fellows let go of the ropes. The horse fell off the rock ledge where they shot him and then he died on a big rock underneath it. They cut him up and took the meat up to my uncle's cave. I and a bunch of boys, we ran up there and somebody took water up there and they boiled that meat. My uncle gave us some. Only a little of it was cooked and he gave us some. It tasted good and I was glad they killed that horse. They took a lot of meat and dried it out in the sun. They hung it across a log. There was blood all over that big rock. Some fellows filled up some guts with blood and took it away. They boiled it and ate it. When I went home, they gave me some more meat and I took it to my mother. She boiled it and I had some more meat. After I ate all that meat, I went swimming with my brother and my cousin. When we were through swimming, we pulled some sweet weeds and ate them and just slept a while in the sun. I sure ate a lot of stuff that time.

When it was fall that year, the teacher took all us old boys to the Valentine School. There was a new school up there. I stayed at that school all fall and my mother cried and cried, because she was scared about me. We had to work in the school for half of every day. Some of the boys worked outside but I had to work in the toilets and clean them up and mop them. I worked in the morning and I went to school in the afternoon. We lived right there at that school in a building and we slept in beds with mattresses and they gave us blankets. I never slept in a bed with a mattress before. I didn't like that bed. I liked the mattress to sleep on but I didn't like the bed. I pulled the mattress off the bed and slept on the floor. Some of us boys did that but the teachers at the school told us not to do that. They said we had to sleep on the beds or they would make us sleep on the floor with no mattress and no blanket. I didn't like the beds because they were high up and if I moved in the bed it squeaked every time. They made us do that. After a while I got used to that bed and it was all right.

Most of the boys didn't fight and they got along all right. We played lots of games and ran races. I didn't do good in those games but I beat the Hualapais in the races. I was a good runner.

The teacher was a woman and they called her Mrs. Rice. The boys up there all said she was all right and they didn't care if they had to be in the school. I was in the fifth grade when I was in that school. When it was New Year the teacher went away and when she came back she made it so I could work in with the blacksmith in Valentine. I liked to work that way. The blacksmith was a Hualapai and they called him Tom. He showed me a lot of things and I liked to be there working with him.

I think most of those boys in that school worked around those places and they didn't care if they had to go to school there. They fed us good and we had lots of meat.

There were three big parts of that school and there was an upstairs too. On one upstairs side, the boys slept and on the other upstairs side, was where the girls slept and there was the places where we went to school underneath. The eating room was in the middle and the principal was there too. One night three Hualapai boys climbed out from a window and they got on the ground. Some girls made a rope from blankets and let it out a window and those boys climbed up where the girls went to bed. They were up there sticking those girls. Some girl saw the boys and she knew who they were and when the next night came she told the principal and he took those boys in the eating room and he tied them up with their hands on the wall and took off their shirts. He whipped them on their backs four times with a blacksnake whip. I could hear him down in that big room and he said a number every time he hit them. He said, "One!" and then he whipped. Then he said, "Two!" and he whipped and he said the number every time. He whipped a boy four times. When he whipped the last boy he said the numbers and he said, "One, Two, Three!: and when he was going to whip the last time I heard that Hualapai boy holler, "Shit! That's enough!"

Those boys came up to the beds and they were crying. I heard one boy cry all night and I didn't sleep much. Nobody talked about it. Nobody said nothing. Those girls they were sticking, they didn't get nothing from the principal and they made the rope for the boys to climb up. Some of us boys were sore at those girls because they didn't get any punishment. I knew girls could make trouble for boys and everyone would say, "That's all right."

The next day a Hualapai man they call Jim, got with us Supai boys near the school and he told us Supais not to do what the Hualapai boys did. He said they were crazy and he said to keep away form those girls and not go near where they sleep. I never did and I don't think the other Supai boys did.

When it was in the first of July, I came home from the school and I was twenty years old then. I was sure glad to see my relatives. I had good clothes on and my relatives sure liked them. My mother said it was good I came home and she cooked a lot of food and she gave me a lot of food to eat. I sure was glad to come down here again. I was always glad to come back down here in the canyon when I go away. I always felt like that. When I am down here I sometimes want to go up on top and go around and see things and work and make money and have good clothes and stuff. I like places out there but I always want to come back down here too. This place here in the canyon is home to me. This is where I can know everyone and every place. Nothing is different or a surprise to me. This is where I can plant a garden. If a man don't plant a garden he has no place. He don't have any part of the ground and no part of his world. A man has to plant a garden. Everybody was living good that time. Everybody had a lot to eat.

I helped my mother in her garden and I worked in my uncle's garden. I just rode around here and I raced my horses for the fun.

Some fellows had some cards and they played gamble when it was afternoon. Lots of men and women all gambled. I didn't know how to do it. I just watched. Nobody showed me how to do it, so I just rode broncos around mostly when those people gambled.

One day Kit Jones and Sinequa gambled in a cave. Sinequa won everything from Kit Jones. He won money and blankets, a saddle and some saddle blankets and a box of bullets. The next day Sinequa went up to where Kit Jones was living to get what he won and Kit Jones told him he couldn't have that stuff and he was sore at Sinequa. Kit Jones was sore footed and he was walking with sticks and he hit Sinequa on the head with a stick. Sinequa hit Kit Jones with his fist and knocked him over and he took all that stuff he won and took it away. Some relatives of Kit Jones told him he shouldn't take it, but he took it. He kept it too.

Sinequa was a good player and one time he played marbles with Supai Shorty and he won a lot of horses from him and a saddle and a bridle. I watched him play with Supai Shorty and he could play good. Shorty let him have all that stuff he won. He said, "You won all this stuff. It's yours now." He wouldn't gamble with Sinequa after that time. Everybody was afraid to gamble with him because he'd win all their stuff. Sinequa went up and gambled with the Hualapais a lot and he always won their stuff. I heard there was lots of trouble about it. I don't know if Sinequa cheated or not but he always won people's stuff.

Sometimes I played marbles with some boys up at the school at the head of the water. I never played for stuff. Only marbles. I never gambled. I never thought I'd like to gamble with those cards. I didn't have stuff to give for when I lost.

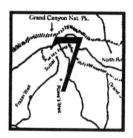

More Dreaming Time—Teddy Roosevelt Comes and Supais Lose More Land

I rode a lot of broncs in that summer and sometimes I dreamed that I was riding with some of my relatives that died. They always said to me, "Let's go swimming - let's go hunt rabbits - let's ride up there and get some horses." I only dreamed about men relatives who died. When I woke up I thought about it and I wondered how I saw those men. I thought they were dead but I saw them just like real. I told my mother, "I saw my relative right here. I know they died but I saw them right here. Did you see them here with me?" My mother told me she didn't see nothing but she said she saw those dead relatives around here sometimes too. She said, "I wonder where they went to."

When I was down here in that summer I dreamed all the time. I dreamed I was up at that school at Valentine. I dreamed I was working around up there. I didn't dream I was in the school. I was just working around up there. I dreamed about those Hualapai boys and I was talking with them. I dreamed about some of those Hualapai girls too, but I never talked to them. They never got close to me when I dreamed about them. I was afraid about dreaming about them and I was afraid of that whip. I kept away from those girls even when I was dreaming.

I got a sore ear in that summer and I didn't hear good in my left ear. If somebody was a little way off and they talked to me, I only could hear, "Wooo-woo-oo." I told my mother I heard something walking around in my ear. I kept hearing it for a month maybe and my ear sure was sore. My mother put some salt and warm water in my ear. I told her I could feel something walk around in that ear and I could feel it come to the top of the water. I said that three times and every time it stopped walking in my ear, so my mother told me not to talk when it was walking up in my ear. I didn't say nothing and my mother put a little stick across my ear hole. After a while I felt that thing walking up in my ear and it came out and pushed the stick away. It was a big tick and my mother killed him. She told me not to let no dogs sleep in my blankets with me. She said, "Don't let no more dogs get in your blankets with you when you're sleeping. Those ticks come from those dogs and they get in your ears." I didn't let no more dogs sleep in my bed with me.

One night I dreamed about two girls. I dreamed I was up there in Coyote Canyon in the winter. Those two girls came to our camp and it was dark and I didn't know who they were. I didn't know if they were Hualapai. They weren't Supai. My mother was there and she said to them, "We got nothing to eat. Only a little piece of meat." Those girls said, "We got some corn in this sack here." When we all ate some corn and some meat the girls went to get some water at a spring with two jugs. They put a saddle on my horse and they took two jugs with them. When they came back from the spring they only had one jug. One of the jugs was broken. My mother said, "How did you break that jug?" One of those girls said, "The string broke and it fell on a rock and broke." My mother said to me, "You go over and lift that other jug off the saddle and don't let it drop and

break it." I got up and went over to get that jug but I woke up
before I got there.

I never dreamed I touched a girl. I always woke up when I
saw them. I never touched them. My mother didn't want me to
get married when I'm young. She said, "You got nothing. You
might starve to death because you haven't got nothing." She
told me not to be after the girls till I'm old enough and I got lots
of stuff so I can get married. My uncle always said that to me
too, so I kept away from girls.

When it was fall my brother, Henry, went up to that school
in Valentine in my place and I went to school down here. When
it was Christmas time my mother went up to Ash Fork for
camping for the winter. I went up there with her. I caught some
horses up there and I hunted for rabbits. I didn't know how to
hunt for deer and I never learned how. I went to the store that
was in Ash Fork sometimes. My mother sold some baskets to
some white people on a train when it was there. She got some
money for those baskets and she gave me some of it and I went
in the store and I got some sugar and coffee and the white man
gave me some apples and some candy. I wondered where the
people on that train came from. I never knew and I never asked
nobody about it.

When it was spring we came home down here. When we
were coming down here we stopped at Rowe's Well for a while
and I hunted for some rabbits up there. There was still some
snow all over and I got snowblind and I didn't see nothing. I
covered my eyes up all the time and I just stayed where it was
dark and I didn't see what I was doing and what I ate. I was that
way for maybe a week and my mother put warm water on my
eyes. When I was all right we came home.

When we got to Hualapai Hilltop, some miners were there.
They had a big barrel and they told me they'd give me a sack of
potatoes and some sugar if I melted snow and filled that barrel

up with water. I stayed up there till I filled it up and they gave
me that stuff. We all liked potatoes and I was sure glad I got
them.

I worked in the garden with my mother and with Hanna
and I went to the school at the head of the water.

That summer the teacher in the school told us the President
of the United States was coming to Grand Canyon (*Ka-thoat-ov-
áh* — big pine — (Grand Canyon before the train) or
(*Wa-poda-cha-wóda* — where a train goes back and forth (Grand
Canyon after the train).[3] All of us boys wanted to see what he
looked like so we went up to Grand Canyon. We camped near
Grand Canyon, and the next day, when it was early in the
morning, a train came and the President got off that train.
Everybody called him Teddy Roosevelt and some people picked
him up and walked around with him and they all clapped their
hands and hollered and we did that too. They walked around
with him and some soldiers walked with him too and then they
took him to the hotel. They took some horses over to the hotel
and Teddy Roosevelt and two men rode by the west rim and I
guess they just went to look.

I sure was glad to see that President. He looked like a good
fellow and I was glad I was seeing him.

When it was noon on that day, we all put some good
clothes and stuff on and we rode over to that hotel and he was
talking to a lot of people. He was standing in the front of the
hotel and he talked to those people. The soldiers stood near him
and they stood straight and they had rifles. I thought maybe
there was a war someplace but I wasn't scared.

I don't know what he was saying but I hollered when the
people hollered and shook some flags around. That night he
went away with the train and some people carried him to the

[3]Theodore Roosevelt visited Grand Canyon on May 3, 1903.

train on their backs. When the train started I was sitting on a fence. Somebody shot off a big gun and it made so much noise, it scared me and I fell off the fence. I think those soldiers shot the gun and I thought there was a war someplace.

When it was night we camped near Grand Canyon and we all said, "We saw the President." Manakadja had a new badge that the President gave him because he was a big chief. He said, "I'm sure glad I got this badge. All the big chiefs got badges."

Teddy Roosevelt said there was going to be a park place at Grand Canyon and there was going to be people there that run it. I asked Manakadja if we were going to get run off this land. Some other fellows asked him if the Supais would get money for the land for the park. That is Supai land and we owned that place they took away. Manakadja told us to wait and see what they do. He said, "I don't think they'll kick us off that land. Captain Navajo told us to wait too. We waited but we got kicked off the land and we didn't get no money for it. We just got kicked off.

School Ends—The Measles Epidemic in 1905

When I came back down here, I went to the school and it was still July. When I went up to the school the teacher told me and three other boys that now we're too old for the school and we shouldn't come up there anymore, so we quit going up there and I never went to school no more. I was in the sixth grade when I quit going.

I was pretty glad not to go to school no more and I could break a lot more horses. I broke eight horses for my cousin, Prince Wodo, in the end of that summer. I sure liked to break horses then. I had nothing to do but break those horses. My cousin said when he's dead I could have all those horses I broke for him. He was a pretty old man and I sure was glad he told me that.

I worked a little down where they had that mine. I washed the dishes those men ate off from and they gave me fifty cents every day I washed them. The man who was boss down there told all the Supai boys they shouldn't come down there but I could go down there because I worked there. I worked there some days for about one month and a half and then the men went up on the Topacoba Trail to fix it better and I quit working.

Some of those Supai boys were sore because those white men said they couldn't go down there where the mine was. They said, "This is Supai land and it is ours and we always go down there when we want to. Those white men can't tell us we can't go where the land is ours. The white men said they had government papers saying that wasn't Supai land no more and only white men could be there. They said if the Supai boys went down there they would make the law make trouble for them. Some of those boys said they wanted to go down there in the night and bust up some of the tools and machines or steal some stuff. They never did. I think they were afraid to get in trouble with the law.

When it was fall, Sinyella told me I could take the mail sometimes to Grand Canyon. He said I could do it two times a week. I had to take the mail up to Grand Canyon and bring it back here the next day. I got one dollar for the whole trip. The government gave Sinyella the money and he paid me. I thought, "If I go to Grand Canyon ten times I'll have ten dollars. That's plenty of money." I told Sinyella I would do that.

When I got the first ten dollars I quit carrying the mail up there and I went to Ash Fork. My mother went with me and we went with Lenomen Sinyella and his wife. They had a buck-board. We camped at Howard Springs when it was night and the next day we went to Ash Fork. My mother had four sacks of peaches and she was going to sell them at Ash Fork. She gave me one sack of those peaches to sell and keep the money. I told my mother, "I got money from carrying mail." My mother said, "If you sell those peaches you'll have more money and you can buy some clothes. I know you got that money. You keep the peaches and sell them and you'll have plenty of money."

My mother traded her peaches for flour and sugar and some coffee. I sold my peaches for some money and I got three dollars and a half and I got some shirts and pants and some boots with that money and the money I got from the mail.

When we came back down here from Ash Fork a lot of fellows wanted to trade some stuff for those boots I got, but I wouldn't trade and I kept those boots.

When it was fall we went to Mohawk Canyon and we camped right there that winter. There was a lot of snow then and we all got cold sometimes. My uncle, Uqualla, got sick when we were there at Mohawk Canyon. He was with us. He just stayed down all the time and he didn't go out. Some Hualapais heard he was sick and they came where we were to see him. Some of them said they were relatives. They said, "He is a good fellow and we're sorry he's sick." Dr. Tommy was a Hualapai doctor and he came and he sang for two or three nights and he made Uqualla a little better. His hot fever was cool a little. When the spring came he was better and he came back down here. He was still sick but he could come down here.

Some boys went to school, but I didn't go. I just helped my mother work in the garden and I broke some horses. I helped my mother and I learned about lots of things in the garden and how to plant the right way. My mother told me not to be lazy and always work in the garden. She said, "Don't run with the girls. Work in the garden and then you'll always have stuff for living." That's what she told me and that's what I did.

One day I got a letter from that blacksmith, Tom, from Valentine. He said there was some kind of sickness in the school and some boys died. He said maybe it was some kind of smallpox and some boys were dead. He said, "Your brother Henry is nearly dead and you and your mother better come to look at him." My mother said she didn't think she could go up there. She said, "That's a hard kind of sickness and the white doctor can't cure it. I'm kind of afraid of it. You go up and see your brother." I said, "I'm kind of afraid I might catch that sickness if I go up there." My mother said, "I don't think you'll catch it if you go up there and see. I can't go when its hot and I'm kind of afraid."

I went up to Valentine and when I got up there, my brother, Henry, was a little better. I stayed at the Hualapais' camp and there was some Hualapais sick too. When those speckles on the sick people went away they went inside. The white doctor told me it was smallpox and when those speckles went away they made a mark on the skin. When measles speckles go away they go off the outside and they don't make some marks on the skin. I stayed up there two days with my brother and he got better, so I came back down here. Some people had that sickness down here when I came back. Nearly all the children had it. They didn't know about the sickness when they jumped in the water when they got all hot from fever and some of them died right in the water and started to float away.

When I got back here the first day, seven of those children died and the next day about twenty more died. Some children died every day and night and after maybe four or five days some grown people got sick and they started to die and after about a week some old people had that sickness and some of them died. After three weeks, nearly a hundred people died[4] and one morning when I woke up, I couldn't breathe good. My breath was hard when it came and I got all hot and the sweat started to come. I didn't go in the water when I was hot. I just laid down. My mother came beside me and cried and she told me my sister, Susie, had the sickness too.

I felt something like ants crawling on my body all the time and when it was the next morning I saw some speckles on me

---

[4]Census data shows 174 as the 1905 Supai population.

and I knew I had that sickness and I said to my mother, "I think maybe I'm going to die. I got that sickness." And then I cried and my mother cried too.

I got hotter and hotter and then I just laid down flat and I saw three roads. They went off in the west. I got up and I walked up the middle road. I looked at myself and I saw I was barefoot and my clothes were only rags. I had some holes in my pants on the knees and my shirt was all torn. I walked on up that road and I could see the land was all flat all around where I could see. I looked all around me and I couldn't see no hills or mountains. It was all flat and I knew I never saw this country before. I thought it was nice and it was pretty to look at. It was cool in that place and I could breathe easy and I wasn't sick no more.

Then I stopped in the road when I heard somebody holler way off ahead of where I was. It sounded like that fellow was hollering across a river but there wasn't no river around there. It was just flat. I heard that hollering and I thought, if I go ahead up there where that hollering is maybe they won't let me come back. I didn't want to go where I couldn't come back if I didn't have some good clothes on. I said, "I want to go back and get some good clothes and my boots and a good hat."

I heard somebody coming in the road so I just laid down in the road and I waited there. Then I saw them looking down at me and there was a lot of them and they all had soldiers' hats on. I thought maybe these are the fellows who I heard hollering and they come to get me. Then it was like waking up in the morning and I saw those people who were looking at me were my mother and some relatives. They just changed and they didn't have no hats on. First they were soldiers and then they were my mother and those relatives. I heard somebody say, "I think he came alive. I think that's what happened." My mother said to me, "I thought you died and I'm sure glad when you showed you are alive."

When I woke up like that I was in my mother's hogan and I asked my mother how I got there and she said I just got up and walked there and she didn't know how I did that when I was sick.

After a few days I got better, but my brother, Joseph, died. He was only a little way off when he died and I saw it. I don't know who took him away and my mother cried a long time. They buried him down by the first falls. They buried nearly all those people who died from that sickness down by the first falls up on the rocks. Lots of people died and there weren't very many left down here then. Most of those people that died were living up by the head of the water or down by the first falls. Most of the people who were left were here in the middle where we live. Nobody sang for those people that died. They just buried them. A lot of my relatives died and I felt like I was more by myself when I knew that. I think it made me scared. The sickness scared me and I was scared that so many of my relatives died.

When I felt like I was better I got on my horse and I rode around down here to see who was still around here. Everybody was crying and they all said, "So many are gone and lots of people are left alone. Some people will take care of themselves after this." Everybody was crying all the time and I could hear it all the time.

Some of the people said the river made the sickness because so many people died when they got in the water and they started to float away. Lots of people wouldn't go in that water no more. They said, "If you step in that water you're going to die." I didn't go in the water for a long time. I just put some water on a piece of cloth and that's how I washed myself.

When I was better I helped in the garden and my mother said, "Lots of people have to take care of themselves now. It's good to work hard so you can take care of yourself."

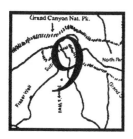

A Lot of Out-of-Canyon
Jobs and More Horses

W hen it was October, I felt strong again like before and I heard maybe I could work up at Rowe's Well (*Haag-ath-gáva* — big lake). I went up there and I worked for Miner Owen and I got thirty dollars in a month. I drove a team and pulled some dirt when they built a dam up there. I worked up there more than two months and Dean Sinyella worked there too. We stayed at Miner Owen's house and he fed us. There was no women there and we cooked for ourselves.

Rowe's Well was near Seligman (*Thahv-ge-ell-élla* — no trees) but I never went in there. "Maybe we might save some money if we don't go in there." That's what I told Dean Sinyella.

Miner Owen had lots of horses all over and some near Williams. They had lots of different brands on them and I thought maybe he stole some of those horses. I never asked him about those horses and he never told me nothing.

When we quit working up there Miner Owen gave us both a bronc to ride back down here to make them gentle. We brought them down here and we rode them around and then we took them back to Miner Owen. I came back down here and I stayed till it was winter.

Before it was winter, lots of Hualapais came down here to race some horses. Captain Jim had a big black horse and he won all the races. Somebody won lots of money. I didn't bet no money but I was wishing I bet on that black horse.

When it was winter, I went up to Mohawk Canyon with Supai Jack and he took his wife. Her name was Lillie. There was lots of snow and rain and when we were up there a few days, she got sick when it was night. She got that sickness lots of people died from before. She had it before but she got it again. She said, "I don't think I'll live for a long while." We watched for her and she just got more sick. She just sat all the time in the hogan and nobody went to sleep. She was like that nearly two weeks I think and one night she died. She couldn't breathe no more. She grunted a while and she died. Supai Jack laid down next to her and he cried till it was morning. When it was morning he stopped crying and he sat up for a while. I just sat there and I didn't say nothing. He got up and went outside. Then he saddled the horses and we took his wife, on one of those horses, about ten miles to someplace where Supai Jack knew there was a cave. We dragged her up to that cave and we put her in there and laid her on her back and then we took off the ropes. We went out of there and Supai Jack said, "Nobody will find this cave."

We rode back where we were camped and Supai Jack cried all night I think, but I was tired so I went to sleep. In the morning we came out of the hogan and Supai Jack said, "I'm worrying because my wife died here. I don't want to stay in this place." We put all our stuff on the horses and we went over to Rowe's Well. We didn't burn that hogan because it was green. We just built it. Supai Jack went back there when it was summer and the hogan was dry and he burned it.

We went over to Rowe's Well and there was lots of Supais over there. Manakadja, Panameda, Supai Charley and my uncle were camped over there. Supai Jack's wife was Supai Charley's daughter and Supai Jack told him she just died and he didn't say nothing. After a while he cried and he went someplace. I wished I could go with him and help him feel better like he helped me when I was scared when I was a boy in Williams. I thought he wanted to be by himself so I didn't try to find him.

Some other people got that sickness again in that winter and some more died. Nobody got those speckles but they were sick on the inside.

When it was spring me and Supai Jack came home down here. Jesus Christ! There was so much mud, Supai Jack's horse got stuck. We took all the stuff off him and we pulled him out with a rope. We got stuck three times when we were coming home. There was mud all over before we got to Hilltop.

I helped my mother plant her garden when I got down here. There wasn't alfalfa then and everybody planted corn all over and that's what we planted. I helped some fellows when they fixed the irrigations ditches too. I just worked around here and I broke some more broncs for my cousin. I wanted to have a real saddle so I gave George Yumiska a horse for a real saddle. I had a horse and a saddle and some blankets and some good clothes, but I didn't think about getting married. My mother told me, "You ride broncs and let those girls alone and it will be better for you." That's what I did.

Some boys asked me how to break broncs. They asked me how do I stay on. I just said, "You hang on with your knees and you watch that bronc's head all the time to see what he's doing." Lots of those boys rode some broncs but they fell off. I was a good bronc rider. Hugh Package-of-Coffee helped me ride some broncs too. He was a good bronc rider and he helped me break some broncs.

When it was late in that summer everything got ripe and we had a ceremonial down here. Some boys made masks to wear and I made a mask from some canvas. I made it look like some ghost. Some of the old men said we ought to make those masks look like ghosts. I made it look like what a ghost maybe looks like. I put leaves all around it and I put leaves on my legs and we did that ceremonial. Sinyella knew all those Hopi mask dance songs. He sang those songs and we danced. He said we should dance and sing for rain and green grass and it will make our land good. We danced in the day like the Hopis.

After we danced it rained so much, part of the canyon got flooded and my uncle's hogan got washed away. Those dances and songs sure made a lot of rain and I was glad. I helped make all that rain when we danced and sang those songs. When I was dancing those dances I didn't think about that rain. I only danced for the fun but when it rained I was glad I was in that singing and dancing.

When it was September my cousin told us, "There's lots of piñon nuts in Mohawk Canyon. We should go get some of those nuts." Lots of Supais went up there. I went up with my mother. I climbed the trees and threw those nuts down for her and we got a lot. We brought them back down here and my mother roasted them and we ate a lot.

I stayed down here a while and then I went back over to Mohawk Canyon. My uncle was over there and I asked him if he wanted me to bring some nuts down here for him but he said, "I got enough," so I just stayed up there a while.

A Hualapai they called Frank Wilder came over to our camp and he said, "I'm going over to Nelson (*Yoo-new-wá*— owl nest) at the Lime Kiln Company and cut some wood over there. They give you money for it over there. I'm going to stay all winter. If you want to come, why don't you come?" I told him, "I'll go with you."

Frank Wilder got a team he borrowed and we went to Nelson and we camped right there. He didn't have no wife and we cooked for ourselves. Lots of people were camped around there and everybody cut wood for the Lime Kiln Company. Most of those people were Hualapais. Everybody made a lot of money but they took a lot of money for food in that store the Lime Kiln had, so there wasn't much money left.

Frank Wilder paid two Mexicans to cut wood for us. We paid them half what we got for that wood when we hauled it in but after a while that Hualapai went off someplace. He said, "I'm going to visit somebody," and he went off but he didn't come back. I thought maybe he was sore at me but I just stayed there and cut a lot of wood and after that those Mexicans ran off.

On day a Hualapai came by there and he said, "I'll give you a mare for all that wood you cut," so I gave him all the wood and I took the mare and then I just stayed around a week and I didn't do nothing. Then I came back down here. When I was coming back here I camped the first night with the Hualapais at Pine Springs. They said, "I thought you were staying at Nelson to cut some wood." I told them, "I quit. I'm tired and I don't make much money over there. I'm thinking about going home." Some of those Hualapais, they told me, "That Hualapai, Frank Wilder, will take you someplace and treat you good and take all your stuff and run off." I told them, "He didn't take my stuff. He ran off but he didn't take my stuff." I stayed up there for two or three days and then I came down here.

All those peaches had flowers when I came down here and I sure was glad of it when I saw that. I was glad I came down here. It was warm but not hot and every place smelled good and it was quiet and I was glad.

I helped my mother plant in her garden and stayed around here till it was May and Supai Jack came over here to my mother's camp and he said, "You and me will go to Seligman."

I said, "Why should we go up there?", and he told me we could get a lot of groceries up there. We got a buckboard from Captain Jim and we used our horses and we made a team for that buckboard and we went to Seligman. We got some sacks of flour and a lot of sugar and some coffee and baking powder and some salt and fifty pounds of potatoes.

When we were coming back down here we stopped by where Miner Owen's place is and we stayed there while it was night. He asked me to break a bronc for him and I said, "I'll do that," so I put a saddle on that horse and he bucked me all over that corral. Jesus Christ, he was the hardest bronc I ever rode and I thought I got throwed off but I was still on. After a while he quit bucking and Miner Owen told us why don't we come up to Williams after a while because we could get some wild horses over there.

We took those groceries to Hilltop and we packed them down here. We sold some of that stuff but we kept a lot of it too.

After a while we went back up there to Williams. We saw Miner Owen right in the town and he took us to his place and he fed us a good meal and we went over to where those wild horses were and we stayed there all night. When it was the next morning, Miner Owen came over there and he had some fresh horses and we rounded up those wild horses and drove them in a corral.

The next day I rode way up where there was a lot of pine trees and I just laid around there by myself for all that day. I liked it there a lot and I said, "Maybe I'll come back here sometime." Then I went back down to Williams to get some money from him for getting those horses. He told us if we stayed up there a month to help him he'd give us thirty dollars. I thought maybe I'd stay up there and get that thirty dollars, so I broke some horses for him.

One day Miner Owens and Supai Jack and two white men went off someplace and they took a lot of whiskey and they drank a lot of that stuff. Those two white men bought all those horses we got for Miner Owen and they didn't pay him only a little money for those horses. They made him drunk when they bought them. We didn't have no more work to do so I came down here. Supai Jack was drunk for a long time and he didn't come down here for a while. I didn't want to see him. I was sore at him.

First Wife and the Great Flood of 1911

When I got down here it was in the middle of June and I worked in the garden mostly. I helped Supai Jack build a hogan after he came back here. I wasn't sore at him no more. We cut some logs up at the head of the water and we dragged them down here and put those logs up and cut some willows for the roof and then we put dirt all over that. When we got it done, I moved my bedding over to that hogan with Supai Jack. We lived there. I told my mother, "Supai Jack hasn't got nobody to live with. I think I'll go live in his hogan with him." My mother said, "That's all right. You go live in that hogan. You can cook now." My mother lived with my brother Henry, then.

When it was fall a Navajo came down here and he had two big blankets and he wanted some buckskins. I had four from my uncle and I traded with that Navajo. I gave him four buckskins for those blankets. After he was gone, a Hualapai came down here. They called him Kate Crozier and he's still alive. He had a rifle and I told him I'd give him one of those Navajo blankets for that rifle, so he came to where I had those blankets and he said the one he wanted. I gave him a blanket and I got that rifle. He said, "When you come to Pine Springs sometimes you hunt deer for us. I got no rifle now to hunt deer. You give us the meat and you can keep the skin." I said, "All right, I'll do that," and I went up to Pine Springs with him. I wanted to try that rifle so I went up there and I killed two deer. I had a hard time to find those deer. I didn't think I'd find none. When I killed them I packed them back to Pine Springs and gave the meat to those people and I got those skins. I brought them back down here and my uncle tanned them for me because I didn't learn how to do it yet. He showed me how to do it, and he said, "You get some more hides and you tan them and you might learn sometime."

My uncle tanned those hides good and he took them up there to Tuba City and he got two blankets for those skins. I wanted to go up there too with him, but he didn't tell me I could go with him. When I got those blankets, I gave one to my mother and I kept one so I had good bedding.

One day an Apache-Mohave (Yavapai) man came down here and he brought his boy with him. They came down here to see Supai Charley. Watahomigie's daughter sure liked that Apache-Mohave boy and she went off with him above the head of the water and I guess he was sticking her. Watahomigie went up there and he made her come home and she cried all the time. She sure liked that boy a lot. Watahomigie's wife said, "Those Apache-Mohaves are bad people and they killed lots of our relatives and she shouldn't run off with that boy." I heard her say that. That's why Watahomigie went after that girl.

When it was the next spring, Lenomen Sinyella married an Apache-Mohave girl and her mother and father and two brothers stayed down here till it was the end of the summer. That girl's father was Jim Ketchum and they stayed with Lenomen Sinyella up at the head of the water. Nobody said nothing about it but nobody liked those Apache-Mohaves because they used to come raiding down here and kill our people and steal our food and stuff.

Up at the head of the water there was a man that lived there. His name was Mus-káh and he lived up there with his woman and they had a lot of boys, but all those boys died and there was only one boy left and they called him George Yumiska and he had a sister. She was Anjelik and I knew that girl for a long time and I liked her all the time. Those people used to camp near where we camped in the winter up at Mohawk Canyon and I liked her. I never talked to her. I just looked at her sometimes. I never said to some other boys, "I'd like to stick her." Some of the other boys talked about some girls and they said, "I'd like to stick that girl." I never said I'd like to stick that girl. I just liked her.

When it was winter, after my uncle got those blankets from Tuba City, I went up there near Pine Springs and I camped with some Hualapais. Anjelik's father and her brother camped up by there too and I heard them say to some of those Hualapais, "Anjelik wants to get married with Mark." I thought about what I heard. I thought about it a lot in that winter.

When it was spring I came back down here and Fred Uqualla told me, "Anjelik likes you and she'd like to get married with you. She likes you pretty good." He said he'd tell her to come up here and get me. I didn't say nothing and he told her to come up where I am. The next day Anjelik came up here to our camp. She came where I was and she said, "Why don't you come over there where I am when it's night? We can stay there and you've got enough stuff for a wife." I told her, "I don't want to be married and I haven't got nothing." She said, "You come over there in the night time and you can stay there." I didn't go over to her place. I just stayed at our camp when it was night and early in the next morning I climbed up on those rocks, but she didn't come over to our camp in the morning. When I came down from there she saw me and she came over and she said, "Why didn't you come over there last night?" I didn't say nothing. I just kept looking at something and I didn't say nothing. She took a hold of me but I made her let go and she kept asking why I didn't go over there to her place when it's night and stay with her. I didn't say nothing and she went away. I didn't go over there.

My mother said, "Why don't you go over there? There's a wife for you and you can have her. She wants you to come. A man should have a wife sometime."

The next morning Anjelik came over to our camp again and I hid up in those rocks and my mother told her where I was. She came up there and she just kept talking to me. She said, "Why don't you come over there tonight. My mother and father want you to come. They say you're a good husband for me." I told her, "I'm afraid to come over there." She said, "It's all right."

When it was night I walked over there to her place. I stood where they couldn't see me and I was looking at the fire and the camp. When everybody went to bed I went up there and sat outside the hogan. Anjelik came out and she said, "Why don't you come inside where I am?" Then she took a hold of my arm and she pulled me in there. I was shaking all over myself and I couldn't say nothing so I just laid down and she was putting her hand on me and it got hard. After a while I took off some of my clothes and I laid close with her and then I stuck it in her. It was all hot there and I was hot all over and I got slippery when I sweated so much. I sure liked that a lot and I didn't shake no more. I never was in between a girl's legs like that before.

I took my bedding over to Anjelik's place and I stayed there till it was winter. After about a week Anjelik had her bleeding time and her mother took her in the river and washed her with soapweed and my mother washed me. That soapweed was bad on me and I got red and spotted all over where I washed with it and my eyes swelled up.

I ran sometimes for four days when Anjelik had her bleeding time. My mother said, "If you don't wash when your wife has her bleeding time, you'll be no good and sleep all the time." She told me to drink warm water or my teeth will fall out.

When she stopped bleeding every time, we took a bath. I took a bath every morning for four days. I always did that when Anjelik had her bleeding time.

When it was winter we went up to Pine Springs and it snowed all the time and that snow was about four feet deep. We stayed with that Hualapai, Kate Crozier, and we hunted some deer, but the snow got deep and then it got warm and it rained all the time for five days. Just rain, not snow. The snow all melted and there was water all over. When it quit raining, me and Kate Crozier went over to Nelson to get groceries. Some Hualapais were over there and they told us a flood washed away everything in Supai. All the hogans. All the crops and some horses and people. The next day we went back to Pine Springs and I told Anjelik what I heard those Hualapais say and we were scared for all those relatives down here, so we got all our stuff and we started to come back down here. We saw some Supais on the Hualapai Trail and they didn't have no bedding. They didn't have nothing. They told us a whole lot of water came down through the canyon early in the morning and it washed everything away. That water all came at one time and it was as deep as way up on the sides of the canyon.[5] They said some people heard that water like it was thunder when it was coming and they hollered and people ran out of their hogans and they just ran up on the cliffs and the water came through and washed away all the hogans and trees and horses and everybody's stuff. It all

---

[5]The flood of January 1911 seems to have reached a crest of as much as forty feet.

went down the river over those falls. They said maybe some people went down the river too.

We came down here to see it and we were scared for all those people down here. There wasn't any trail and we just went over rocks and we saw where the schoolhouse used to be, there is just some stones. The white people didn't have no clothes and the buildings were all gone. The agent was Mr. Coe and he only had his underwear and one shoe and the lady had his nightshirt. They didn't have nothing else. Nobody had nothing left. No houses and no crops. They told us an old blind lady just stayed in her hogan when the water came and she went over the falls. Some fellow saw her hanging in a tree down there below the falls and she was dead.

Nobody had nothing to eat. Some people found some sacks of flour from where the government had them in a building that got washed away. Some of those sacks of flour got caught in some trees and brush and that's all there was to eat. All those horses and colts that got drowned got rotten and the meat wasn't good to eat.

Everybody stayed up by those ruins near the Apache Trail and they were afraid maybe there'll be more flood. After a while everybody had a meeting up there by that place and that white man, Bass, wrote on a piece of paper what he saw about the flood and all the stuff gone - the horses and hogans and corn. He sent that paper to the government and he said we wanted some groceries and some tools and some bedding. After maybe two months all that stuff came down here. Every man got one shovel and a pick and a hoe and a plow and a pitchfork and a rake and some bedding. Everybody got two sacks of flour and five bags of coffee and some sugar and beans and salt. When we waited for that stuff to come we didn't have nothing. We ate squirrels and weeds for a while.

Everybody was afraid to come down off those high places. They were scared maybe more water might come down here and maybe they'll be drowned and lose all their stuff. Me and Anjelik and my mother and Hanna stayed up on a high place over a year. Hanna was old and he couldn't do much and I helped him.

The Marriage Ends

When it was summer that year, I tanned lots of hides and my uncle showed me how to do it good. I tanned eight or nine hides. My uncle told me, "When you learn how to tan those hides good, don't let nobody help you when you do it and then you got those hides for yourself." He showed me how to use the brains of the deer to rub into the hides to make them white. Supai hides are white and that is why everybody wants to trade for them.

I kept all those buckskins for myself and I just waited for the Navajos or the Hopis to come down here. When Anjelik saw those buckskins she said, "We'll get along pretty good now." She said she was glad for me to be her husband and she got along good with those people in my camp and she wanted a baby too, but she never had one. She never had a baby with any other man neither.

I didn't trade any of those buckskins that year. I just kept them and I waited till I could make some good trading with the

Navajos or the Hopis. There was a few peach trees left from the flood and when those peaches got good to eat we had a ceremonial down here and some Navajo boys came down here, but they only came to the dance and they didn't have nothing so I just kept those buckskins.

Manakadja was big chief and he talked to lots of people about making another schoolhouse. Everybody said, "Don't have that schoolhouse near the head of the water like it was before." They wanted to put it on Rock Jones' land, but he said he didn't want no school on his land. He said that school was all right up at the head of the water, but Manakadja said its too far away. Rock Jones said he wanted money for that land if they put a schoolhouse on his land. He said he should have fifty dollars for that land and that's what the government gave him and they put that schoolhouse on his land. They put it up there and the roof was only a tent and that's where they went to school.

The new teacher was a good fellow and he gave out lots of food for people. I don't remember his name. In that summer they started to build the agency too on some of that land and I helped them to get some rocks for the bottom of the building.

When it was winter me and my wife went up to Pine Springs and I built a hogan up there and that's where we stayed and I hunted all the time. I got five deer that time. There wasn't very much snow. Just a little on the ground sometime. It made it so I could track deer easy. We didn't see nobody for all the winter and I liked to have it that way. Nobody came there where we were and we didn't go no place and we just stayed there alone.

When it was spring we came back down here and I started to tan all those buckskins and I worked in the garden too. I stretched those buckskins as much as I could do it. I made them long and wide and white and that's how the Navajos and the Hopis like them. I worked on those skins and I worked in the garden all the time.

When it was July I went up to Kingman and there was a rodeo up there and that's what I went up there to see. After that rodeo I came back down here and my mother told me, "Your wife doesn't stay with us. She's no good. She doesn't stay with us. She's run off with two men. She ran off with Richard Siyuja and Mexican Jack. She ran off with both of them." Hanna said that was true. He said she liked those men and she went with them. I didn't say nothing. I just thought maybe she was crazy. I don't know why she ran off with those men. I guess she just liked them. I didn't say nothing to nobody about that. She came to my place and she got her stuff and went to her mother's place and I didn't see her and I didn't say nothing. I saw Mexican Jack and Richard Siyuja, but I didn't say nothing to them. I thought, "If they want that girl they can have her and I don't want her no more." Then I went up to Nelson with some Hualapais and I wanted to work somewhere up there. I cut some wood for four days by Nelson and I thought about Anjelik sometime and I was sorry she was gone and I don't have a wife no more.

Some Hualapais told me there was some place to work over by Jerome and I could pick peaches and lettuce and toma-toes over there and they pay pretty good. I went over there to Jerome on a train. I never was on a train before and I thought maybe it would come off the tracks and I was scared some. I didn't like all that noise. I didn't know that train went so fast. I never moved so fast before. Sometimes I did in a dream.

Supai Jack was living over there by Jerome with that Apache-Mohave woman and that's where I stayed. I picked stuff and I hoed weeds and I wished my wife was up there sometime but I didn't think about her much. Sometimes in the night time I could hear Supai Jack and his Apache-Mohave wife when they were together in their bedding. Then, sometimes, I wished my wife was with me in my bedding.

When I was up there about two months, I heard from Supai and my mother said I should come back down here because

Hanna died and she's by herself. When I got some money I came back here. I got on that train and I went to Nelson and I got my horse and I came down here.

I sure was sorry I didn't see Hanna before that. He was a good fellow and he took care of us good. I sure was sorry he was dead. Hanna wasn't my real father but I could remember him from when I was little and he always treated me and my brothers and my sister, Susie, good and he was good to my mother and I know she liked him and I was sad about him dying.

After I was down here a week maybe, Anjelik came over here and she tried to get in my bed again. I said, "I don't want you back here no more. You're no good. You run around with those other fellows. You like those other fellows sticking you. You go with them. I don't want you." She didn't say nothing. She went away and stayed with her mother. I stayed with my mother awhile and I helped her with her garden. My mother said, "It's good you don't have that girl back here. She's no good for you. I thought she was a good girl and a good wife for you but she's bad. Let those other men have her."

When it was fall I went to Nelson again and I cut wood till it was winter, then I went to Kingman and I stayed with a Hualapai relative. I worked there in that winter. I dug some holes for houses the white people were making. I did that all winter. I hunted some rabbits too and that's what we ate.

When it was almost spring, I went back there to Nelson and I borrowed a horse from some Hualapais and I went over to Mohawk Canyon. My mother and Susie and Susie's husband were over there and that's where I went. I said, "I want a horse so I can go back over there to Nelson and get my bedding. I want to come back here." I stayed over there about a week and then I went and got my bedding and I gave that Hualapai his horse and then I went back to Mohawk Canyon and I took my bedding. I just stayed there and I hunted for some deer but I didn't get one.

After a while we came back down here and some people told me, "Anjelik is married with a Hualapai and she's gone with him up by Seligman. That's where they're living." I wasn't sorry she was gone any more. I didn't care if she wasn't around. Nobody said nothing about it.

When it was August that Hualapai, Kate Crozier, said for me to come up there to Pine Springs and help him build a log house for him to live in. I went up there and I helped him cut some logs and peel them and haul them and then we built that place. Then I came back here and I lived with my sister, Susie. She told me the government sent some wooden houses out here and if somebody goes up to Seligman and hauls them down here and puts them up he can have that house. She said they sent five houses out here and some Supais got four already. Kit Jones wanted that other house but he didn't have no team to bring all that wood back here. Susie told me, "You get that house and we'll have it." Susie's husband, Supai Charley said, "I'll help you get that house."

I got a team from my brother and I used that government wagon up at Hilltop. Supai Charley didn't come up there with me and I drove that team to Seligman alone. When I got there, Jesus Christ, it began to snow a lot and nobody thought it would snow so early.

I camped up there and when it was morning I put some stuff on the wagon and I couldn't get those horses to pull because the wheels were frozen on the ground. I chopped it loose and I got to Rowe's Well. I went early in the morning from there and when it got warm a little everything was mud. Before I got to Hilltop that wagon got stuck in mud and the horses couldn't pull it out. I whipped those horses and I pulled on them and I pushed the wagon but I couldn't get that wagon loose.

After a while I sat on the wagon and I thought, "How can I get this loose?" I heard somebody coming and I said, "I hope I will get some help now." When he got up close, I saw my brother was coming. We got that wagon loose form the mud and I hurt my eyes from the sun on that snow. When we got that wood down here I got snowblind. I just stayed in the hogan for a while and my mother put warm water and salt on my eyes. When I got better I went and got some more of that house and my brother helped me. Kit Jones wasn't sore because I got that house. All those Supais that got those houses helped put them up and everybody helped everybody.

After I got that house put up, Kate Crozier sent me sixty dollars because I helped him put up that log house. I felt rich when I had that money and I thought, "Maybe I'll get some more." I told my mother, "I'm going up there to Jerome and I'm going to work with Supai Jack and pick some stuff." I liked to go out of here sometimes and get some of that money. I never stayed out of here for a long time. I always came back and saw if my mother was out of food or some wood and I helped in the garden. I liked to go out and work for money and then I can buy stuff. When I got money I feel like its all right and I can buy stuff. Sometimes I don't like to eat corn all the time and I can buy groceries when I've got some money and I can get some stuff for my mother and I can get some good clothes. When I've got good clothes I don't feel like a poor boy. I thought maybe if I got good clothes maybe some girls would like it and they'd want to marry with me, but I won't marry them. I just wanted them to wish I'd marry them, but I wouldn't do that. I never thought, "I'd like to have that woman with me." Only sometimes when I'm laying in my bed. Then sometimes I thought, "I'd like to have a woman in my bed with me right now", but when the sun came up I was glad I didn't have that woman with me.

Supai Charley is Murdered and Anjelik Dies—Mark Marries Again

When I was working up on top with Supai Jack, I was pulling some stuff with a team and it hit something like a rock and I fell and I hurt myself in my side. I just stayed in bed at Supai Jack's place a week maybe and he put some liniment on me and I got better and then I worked with the railroad and shoveled a lot of stuff.

When it was the end of June, I had some money and I quit working and I went back to Williams and I saw that rodeo there when they had the Fourth of July. There was some Supais there and we saw that rodeo and some races. I tried to climb up a greased pole and get five dollars and I tried to catch a greased pig and get five dollars. Everybody tried to get that pig but nobody did. I saw a bronc buster there. He was a white man and he just looked around and he smiled when that horse was bucking. He didn't watch the horse and I was wondering how that fellow stayed on the horse when he didn't watch that horse. Jesus Christ, he was a good rider.

Some white man up there told me he'd give me fifty cents a head if I'd bring twelve horses over there. I did that and I got the money. Then I came home down here and I helped my mother in her garden. I helped some boys down here to learn about riding broncs.

I was kind of sorry I was down there in that summer and I was glad when I heard about a job to dig out a spring up at Howard Springs. I went up there and I took some boys with me. I took Bela Wescogome and Lemuel Paya with me and they were glad to go out of here and see some things. They worked all the time, but they were glad to get out there and see some things.

When that spring was dug out, those boys went to Pine Springs to break some horses and I came back down here. I helped the teacher make some bricks for a chimney. I had to help him do that because he helped me when I was putting up that wooden house. I had to help him because he helped me. I ate some food with him once and he gave me some chicken to eat. I sure liked that chicken. He gave me some fish from a can once too and I ate it.

A Hualapai, Frank Cook, said I should come up there to Pine Springs and help him round up some steers and he can sell them. I said, "I'll go up there." My cousin said, "Why don't you stay down here sometime?" and I told him, "I've got no money now and I want to get some money and I can buy a new saddle and my mother can have some of that money."

I went up there to Pine Springs and I roped those big steers. I never roped big ones like that before and I got scared a little sometimes. I was kind of afraid but I wanted to have that money so I roped them and we rounded them up. When Frank Cook sold those steers he got some money and he went with some white boys in Seligman and they got drunk. I took the saddle horses back to the Hualapai camp and I was glad I didn't get drunk and go in Seligman with those fellows. I didn't like to be drunk and get trouble from that. I never like to get so I don't know where I am or what I'm doing. I see those Indian boys get drunk and I don't want get like that. I just stayed at that Hualapai camp and some Hualapai relatives said, "Why don't you stay up here and hunt some deer?" I liked to stay with those Hualapais. They wanted me to stay and I wanted to have some buckskins. My sister, Susie, traded all those buckskins I was saving. She took them all up to Tuba City and she traded all those buckskins I had. She needed to have all that stuff she got.

I went to hunt for deer with those Hualapais and I only got three. I took the skins and I ate some of that meat and I brought a lot of meat down here for my mother and my sister. My mother was sure glad of it when I brought that meat down here. She said, "I like you to bring me this stuff. I like this meat and stuff better than when you give me money."

I worked on those hides but it got cold down here and I didn't finish, so I broke a colt from that mare I got from cutting wood and I just rode that horse around and made him gentle. I finished one of those hides and Supai Charley took it to Tuba City and he got a big blanket for it.

When it was winter Supai Charley and my sister, Susie, were camping up at Hilltop and that's where they stayed all winter. When it was spring, Supai Charley got some cattle and he killed a calf he owned and that's what they had for some meat. One day a white man they called Jim Black came around with a cowboy they called Bill Norton. They came around that camp where Susie and Supai Charley were and they saw that calf hide where it was spread on the ground where the sun can dry it, and they thought Supai Charley killed a calf from Jim Black's steers. Supai Charley didn't have no brand on it and that's what those fellows thought. They went over to Rowe's Well and told some cattlemen over there, a Supai killed a calf up there at

Hilltop. Then Jim Black went out and he shot an old cow dead and he cut off its head and he took that head up there to Flagstaff and he told the court up there Supai Charley shot that cow and he ate him and they saw him eating that cow. That's what he told to Tom Pollack, the banker that owned lots of steers around there, and they got a policeman and they went and got Supai Charley and put him in that jail in Flagstaff.

After a few days, Bill Pitts went up there to Flagstaff and he paid some money and Supai Charley came out of jail and he went back to his camp at Hilltop but they came back and got him and put him in that jail again. The floor was all wet in that place and Supai Charley had no place to sleep so he had to lay in that water. He was in that place about four days and then he died from being wet all the time.

When lots of Supais heard about Supai Charley died in that jail, we went up there and we wanted to have Supai Charley's body and Susie came up there with us. Everybody was sore and we wanted to have Supai Charley's body but they already buried him when we got up there to Flagstaff in a graveyard. Some men showed us where they put him and we dug him up.

Jesus Christ, when we got that coffin dug up it was all rotten and I said, "Maybe we dug up somebody else." Some Supais opened that coffin up and Supai Charley was in there. They just put him in a rotten coffin. He didn't have no clothes on and some white man had put red paint on his face and they put some chicken feathers in his hair. We knew some white man did all that stuff for making a joke. All those Supais were pretty sore.

Bill Pitts gave us a big box and we put Supai Charley in there and covered him good and nailed that box shut tight. Bill Pitts let us use a buckboard and we took him to Howard Springs and when we came in there lots of Supais were there and everybody was sore and there was lots of crying and everybody

Mark Hanna at 72
(1953)

Cataract (Havasu) Canyon

(Emerick Photo)

Northern View

(Emerick Photo)

Southern View

Mooney Falls (220 feet)
Havasu Canyon

Mark Hanna at 72
(1953)

Susie Hanna at 90
(1953)

(Emerick photo)

Traditional Havasupai House
(1950)

(Emerick photo)

Havasupai Sweat House
(1950)

Watahomigie's wife, Mamie
(1953)

Lina Iditicava at corn grinder
(1953)

Captain Navajo
(Late 19th-Early 20th Century)

(Photographer unknown)

Mark Hanna with Doc Pardee's Wild West Show
(Early 20th Century)

Supai Charley
(Early 20th Century)

Mexican Joe
(Early 20th Century)

Man of the Canyon

was worrying about it. All those Supais liked Supai Charley and he was a good fellow.

Bill Pitts let us take that buckboard to Hilltop and then lots of Supai boys carried Supai Charley down here and they took him down by the first falls and everybody went down there and there was a big sing for one day and that night and everybody cried. Supai Jack's father knew some of those Hualapai and Mohave songs for dead people and he sang lots of those songs.

Everybody was sore at those white fellows and some Supais said, "We're going to kill some white fellows. Those two fellows Jim Black and Bill Norton, we're going to go up there and kill those two fellows." They were just talking. They didn't kill nobody.

Susie said she was going up and shoot Jim Black when he was away from his place. She said, "I'm going to get a gun and I'll shoot him up there." That's what my sister said, but she didn't go up there and she didn't kill nobody. I didn't say nothing to her.

They buried Supai Charley down by the first falls but I wasn't there when they buried him. I went up to Bill Pitts and took that buckboard back there.

I heard that Kate Crozier had his wife die and he wanted me to come up to Frazer Wells and stay with him and cut some wood for the white men up there. I went up there and he just cried all the time because his wife died. I felt sorry because he lost his wife and he was worried for her.

When I was up there I heard about Anjelik, that she came back down here to Supai and she got sick down here and she died and I wasn't sorry about that. I was glad about it when she died. She was looking for how to go away from me and she died and she's gone away for always and I was glad about it. I told some people I was sorry, but I was glad. I didn't cry. I was just thinking I was glad.

After we cut that wood at Frazer Wells I went over to the Hualapai camp by Nelson and I stayed there all winter. One of those Hualapais, Frank Wilder, told me, "One of these girls wants to be married with you." Every time I saw that fellow he said, "Why don't you come over that girl's place? Her father wants you to come over there and stay with her and be married with her." I didn't say nothing. He just told me that every day. I was staying with that Hualapai doctor, Doctor Tommy, and he said, "Why don't you go over and get that girl and bring her to this place and she can cook for us?" That girl's name was Toddy and I told him, "I don't want to be married with that girl, Toddy. I'll just go over there and look at her but I don't want to be married with her." Doctor Tommy told me, "Go over there and get that girl. She's all right."

After a few days I went over to near where her camp was and I saw Frank Wilder and he said, "You stay here and be with this girl. Her mother and father want you to stay with her and that girl wants to be married with you." I said, "No, I don't think I want to be married with her." Then Frank Wilder told me, "You're just saying that." His wife told me that too. When the sun was going down I said, "I'm going", and they said, "No, you stay here with us", and then they gave me some food to eat. When I ate that food I said, "I'm ready to go now." When I went outside I saw my horse was turned loose and Frank Wilder had the saddle off and the horse was way off. I said, "Why did you turn loose my horse?" He said, "You ought to stay here and make a place with that girl. She wants to be married with you and her father's got a lot of wood to haul and he needs some help. Go over there now. She's waiting for you now and she wants you to come over there."

I got my bridle and I went after that horse and Frank Wilder ran after me and he took that bridle and ran off with it. I just stayed there with Frank Wilder and his wife and I was kind of afraid to go over there so I just stayed at Frank Wilder's place. I just laid down near the stove and he kept saying, "Why don't you go over there?"

After a while I went over there to that girl's place and they lived in a tent so I went inside that tent. Her father and mother were laying down already to bed on the side of the tent. When I went in there I sat down near her head where she was laying down. I sat there by her a while and I was cold and I was shaking. She didn't say nothing to me and I didn't say nothing. I put my hand on her head and I touched her head and she looked at me and I didn't say nothing. After a while I said, "I got no bedding. Can I come in your bed?" She didn't say nothing for a while. Then she said, "Yes." I didn't go in there with her. After a while she said, "Why don't you come in these blankets with me?", but I didn't get in there with her. Then I took off my shoes and I got in the blankets where she was and I got warm but I just laid down. I didn't do nothing with her. I didn't even touch her. I was afraid. I just laid there all night and I slept but I didn't touch her.

When it was still early and dark in the morning she was sleeping and I got out of those blankets and I went over to Frank Wilder's place. He got up and he made a fire and he said, "Did you bed with her? How was she? What did she say to you?" His wife said to him, "Shut your mouth and don't say things like that!" He said, "I want to know if she was all right when you bedded with her." His wife said, "You don't ask those things from him." She said to me, "You've got a good wife now."

When I ate I went outside and I told frank Wilder, "I'm going away now." He told me, "No, you can't go now." I helped him pile wood all day and when it was light I went over to Toddy's place and I went in that tent. She was in her bedding and I didn't say nothing to her and I wasn't shaking. I just took off my shoes and I got in her bed with her and she was sure good for sticking and I did that all night.

When it was morning her father said, "I don't want you to go. You've got a place now. I told those Hualapais to send you over here for you to stay with this girl. I need you to help me haul wood and pay some stuff I owe in the store. You help me now. You've got a place now and you stay with this girl. You'll be all right now." I said, "Its all right," and I stayed there. I didn't say nothing to that girl. I just ate and I helped with that wood.

When it was night again a hard wind started to blow and it got harder and harder and after a while it tore down all the trees and all those tents and hogans and it blew everything away. We just laid down all night and hung on to stuff. I never saw a wind like that before and it blew all night and all next day. We just laid there and a big piñon tree almost fell on us and I thought maybe we'll get killed.

When the wind stopped after a while, we got up and all those Hualapais tents and stuff were all blown way off and nobody could find some of it. All the trees were blown over and a lot of stuff was gone.

I just kept hauling wood for Toddy's father. I used his wagon but I used my team. I took that wood to the Lime Kiln Company and they gave credit for it in that store. We got stuff in that store and Toddy cooked all that food for us and she could cook it good. I was glad I got married with her. We cut a lot of wood and we paid all that credit in the store and we got forty dollars extra. Toddy's father, Charley Crozier, gave me twenty dollars from that money.

Another Marriage Ends—Dreams and Serious Injury

I heard I could do some work in Ash Fork and get some more money. I heard Bill Pitt in Ash Fork wanted somebody to help him make some cement. I told Charley Crozier and he said, "Where are you going when you don't work over there no more?" I told him, "I'm coming back over here." He said, "It's all right. You can go."

I came back down here before I went over to Ash Fork. I brought some hides down here so my sister can sell them. When I was coming by Frazer Wells all those pine trees were blown over and broken and I heard they had a big wind over there too.

When I came down here I told my mother, "I'm married to a Hualapai girl." She said, "That's good you are. Why didn't you bring her down here?" I told her I was going to stay up by Ash Fork and work for Bill Pitt. My mother said, "Are you going to take that girl over there?" I said, "No, I'm going to stay up there by myself and Bill Pitt is a friend and he'll give me good food. When I'm through work over there I'm going back to where Toddy is." My mother said, "Its all right." I stayed down there in Supai for a week and I helped my brother with some alfalfa. Then I went up there to Ash Fork.

When I got to Ash Fork I went to Bill Pitt's ranch he calls Gold Trap, and he told me to come back down here and get two boys to come up there and help me build a cement tank.[6] He said he wanted me to get Bela and Lemuel and that's who I got down here. We stayed in a tent and Bill Pitt gave us lots of good food. We cooked for ourselves and we even had a lot of meat and we didn't pay for nothing. We got all that stuff from Bill Pitt. I sure liked it there at Gold Trap and I was sorry when we got finished making that tank. We got about seventy dollars from Bill Pitt and then I told those boys, "I got a wife over by Nelson and I'm going over there and see my wife."

I went over to Seligman and I got money for that check I got from Bill Pitt. Then I went to Nelson. I went to where Toddy's father, Charley Crozier, was camped. Nobody was there and some Hualapais told me those people went over by Peach Springs and they're cutting wood for the school. That Hualapai said, "That girl don't want you no more. She said she sent a letter to Ash Fork and she wants money but she never got that money." I told that fellow, "I never got nothing," and he said, "She sure don't want you no more. She's really sore about that money."

On the next day I went over there by Peach Springs. I found where Charlie Crozier was camped and I went over there and it was time to eat but they didn't give me nothing so I went to another Hualapai camp and some people gave me something to eat. When I was done eating I went back to Charley Crozier's camp. Those people didn't even talk to me. When it was night I didn't go into Toddy's bed. I just slept outside by myself. All

---

[6]An artificial water-hole for stock.

night I was thinking about it and I was thinking, "I'll go home. If that girl don't want me I don't care much about her." I thought, "If she wants me I'd stay married with her but she don't want me, so I'll go home."

When it was still dark, I got up and I put my bedding on my horse and I just went off. I went to another Hualapai camp where Auggie Smith was and they gave me some food and some stuff to eat when I'm coming home. His wife said, "What did that girl say to you?" I told her, "I didn't say nothing to her. I'm just going home." Auggie Smith's wife shook her head and he said, "There's girls all over here. You don't have to worry about them. There's plenty." I told her, "I don't want no more girls and no more wife because they're trouble for me."

I went away from Peach Springs and I went to Pine Springs and stayed there at night. The next day I came down here and my mother said, "Did you go see your wife?" I told her, "Yes, I went to see her but she don't want me no more." My mother said, "She wanted you pretty bad but now she don't want you no more. Is it like that?" I said, "Yes, that's why I'm coming home." She said, "Its all right." She said, "A lot of girls are like that now. They don't want to stay with one man very long. They get in one man's bed and stay for a while and then they go with some other man. Girls didn't used to be like that and they get around too much now. That's why there is trouble."

I helped my mother in her garden and I sure was glad I was home down here. I worked on my hides too and I tanned them up and I knew how to do it good. I didn't sell any of those hides. I just saved them. The Hopis and the Navajos didn't come down here much anymore. A lot of them used to come down here but they don't come no more. There's too many other things to do and too many places to go around to.

When I was down here then I didn't pay no attention to nobody. I didn't talk to nobody. I just talked to a few boys I was good friends with and I went swimming with them and I took sweat baths with them. I didn't know those sweat bath songs good then and somebody always sang in there and I listened and sang with those boys and I learned some of those songs.

One night I was laying in my hogan and there was a fellow laying in there right next to me. It was dark in that hogan and I couldn't see who that fellow was. I felt some hand touch my body and I told that fellow that was laying there, "Somebody is in this place touching me." I grabbed that hand and the fingers got all long and big and I bent them like rubber and they wouldn't go away. I yelled to that other fellow and he looked at me and I could see his eyes and he laughed and laughed and those fingers I grabbed got bigger and longer and they were just like hot rubber. I yelled some more and then I woke up and nobody was around there. I was just dreaming but it was all like real.

One other time I dreamed the canyon got all narrow and I was down here and I heard a train coming and I was wondering how a train come down here. I heard that train get louder and louder and I started to yell because I couldn't get out of the canyon and it was narrow. I just yelled and I ran and I was looking for someplace to get out of the canyon before I got ran over by that train. I found a little place on the wall and I climbed up there and I got up there when the train was just going to run over me. I saw that train go to the top of the first falls and it stopped right there and I saw some white people in that train. I saw them get out of the train and walk around. I woke up then.

One other time I dreamed I saw a lot of rubber men. I see rubber men lots of times when I dream. I never see all of the rubber men. I only see parts of them and they always scare me. I usually see their hands and feet.

When it was fall, I heard from a white man they called Bunk Grove. He saw me when I was up there near Ash Fork at Gold Trap, when he was looking for land around there. He told me to come up there and help him clear some land and I'd get some money for that.

When I was going up there to Ash Fork my old uncle said, "I want to go up there too." He went up there with me. He just wanted to ride along. We went to Bunk Grove's place and we stayed there one night and my uncle wanted to go in Ash Fork and buy some groceries. I took him over there. He got some salt and some coffee and a sack of flour. He didn't look around the town much. He just went in that store and got that stuff and we went back to Bunk Grove's place. My uncle stayed there that night and then he came back down here alone. I didn't worry about him. I just told him, "Don't have trouble when you're going down there. Don't get lost." Bunk Grove said he was worrying that something might happen because he's so old. My uncle told him, "It's all right. I can do this all right and I'll get down there." He came down here all right and he didn't get lost.

I worked up there with Bunk Grove and we cleared up eight acres when it was spring. When we got all that land cleared off we plowed it up and then we planted some corn. That's all we planted. Just corn and some beans. Some of those trees we cut down, we hauled in with a team and we cut them all up and made a fence around that land. We made a dirt tank for horses and that's all we did. Then we cut some more of that wood for selling and he got some money for that. I'm a good woodcutter and I cut and peeled maybe fifty fence posts in one day. I stayed there about four months and then I worked for Bill Pitts till it was winter.

When it was May, in the next year, I was at Bunk Grove's place again and I was feeding up that team to plow and I put those horses in the corral and there was just one post in the fence. When they were eating I was standing on that post and then one of those horses kicked the post and I fell a long way and that post hit my chest. I was dead maybe five hours and they couldn't get me alive again. Bunk Grove's wife poured some water on me but I was dead and there was nothing running in my arms.

When I was dead I was a great big man and I just sat down and when I looked around and I saw the trees were all like little weeds around me. Then those trees just turned into little men and all those little men just ran around me and looked way up at me and they laughed and yelled. I thought, "Maybe I'm dreaming." I tried to wake up but I couldn't.

After a while all those men were gone and then lots of little pieces of stone rolled down all around my feet and then all those pieces of stone were little men again after a while and they all ran around me and laughed and laughed when they looked at me but I didn't say nothing. I just sat and looked at them and I was wondering what kind of men they were and why they were laughing at me. They all went away and then I came alive and I was in my bed at Bunk Grove's and he was sitting on my bed and his wife was there too. Bunk Grove got his face way down by my ear and he said my name, "Mark". I couldn't say nothing but I turned my head and I looked at him. I heard Bunk Grove's wife say, "He's all right."

After a while I got up and she gave me some coffee but I was feeling my arm dropping down and I felt something broke in my shoulder and it let my arm go down. Then Bunk Grove fixed my arm on my body and he took me in Ash Fork in a wagon and took me to where that white doctor was. That doctor put his knees in my back and pulled my shoulder and got that broken bone smooth. Then he put that plaster on me and I laid down in someplace and they gave me food and they gave me breakfast when it was morning. That doctor put some more plaster on me and he said, "You leave that stuff on you for one month." I said, "I want to go home and I want to know how much money I should give you." He told me I should give him ten dollars. I only had five dollars and he took it.

I went back over there to Bunk Grove's place and Jesus Christ, it was hard to sleep with that plaster on me. When it was morning I told Bunk Grove, "I want to go home", and he saddled my horse and I went over to a place where Mack Putesoy was working and I told him, "I want you to take me down there to Supai. I got hurt on my shoulder and I want to go home." He asked his boss if he can take me down there and he said it was all right. When it was the next morning we started to come down here and we camped at Howard Springs for the first night and I hurt all over me and I didn't sleep.

When it was the next day we came down here and I went where my mother was. When I was riding in some boys were hollering and they said, "I guess you lost your arm. How did you cut if off? I want to see how you cut it off." I told them, "I just broke it."

An Anthropologist Comes to the Canyon— Mark Works at Many Jobs

I just laid around and I didn't do nothing. When it was the next month my sister cut that plaster off with a knife and she made me a sweat bath and I went in that sweat bath every day and I got better and I rode around a little bit.

When it was August I was in the hogan laying down and a white man came in there and he asked me how do I feel.[7] I told him, "I been sick and I'm just laying down here." He said, "I'm going to help you and you'll have something to do." He told me he wanted me to tell him some things and some old stories. He said he's going to have old Sinyella around there too. He said, "We're going to work tomorrow and Sinyella and Manakadja are going to work too."

When it was the next day we started that work and he asked us all kinds of stuff about bows and arrows and how to

<hr />

[7]The anthropologist, Leslie Spier from the American Museum of Natural History, first visited the Havasupai in August, 1918. He returned in August 1919 and again in 1921. Mark was employed primarily as an interpreter.

make dresses and britches from buckskin and how to tan hides and everything else like that. I didn't think maybe I could talk English good enough but he said, "It's all right."

They called him Spier and he asked us a lot of stuff about all the things the old people used to do. I worked for him for a month. I thought it was good for me to get that money from him because I needed to have it. He gave me a check for that money and when I was through working for him I went up to Ash Fork and I got that money Bunk Grove was going to give me when I worked up there. He was glad when I came up there and I told him I was feeling good and he asked me if I had enough money down there and I told him that white man Spier gave me that check. I showed that check to Bunk Grove and he said, "It's all right."

Bunk Grove gave me my money and I went to Ash Fork and I cashed that check from Spier and I had lots of money and I thought, "I'm rich now." I bought some good clothes and I went back to Grove's place and he said I should come back there in September. Then I came back down here.

The agent down here told us about some war there was around and he said maybe sugar and flour will be hard to get down here and we could only have a little bit of it. He told us this before I got my arm hurt and he was talking about it a lot and he said we should sign some papers about the war and I thought the war was pretty bad and I thought, "Maybe I'm going to where they got that war" and I was scared about it. I thought about those soldiers I saw at Grand Canyon and I thought about those uniforms and I was kind of scared.

When I came back down here from Ash Fork I just helped my mother with her corn and her beans and pumpkins.

When it was September I went back to Bunk Grove's and I cut some oats up there for him. Dudley Manakadja went up there with me and he helped me cut those oats. When we got through up there I went over to the Hualapai camp by Ash Fork and Dudley Manakadja came down here.

When I was with those Hualapais, Lemuel Paya came up there and he said he's going to work over by Howard Lake to load sheep shit on some railroad cars. I said, "Maybe I'll go over there too and I'll get a little money." It sure was hard to load that shit on those cars and it smelled real bad. The wind blew that shit all over us and we always smelled like sheep. We quit doing that after maybe two weeks and we had to clean up a long time to get that sheep shit off us.

I went back over with those Hualapais near Ash Fork and I cut some wood over there and they gave me some food. Then I went back to Bill Pitts' place and Lemuel Paya was there and I was coming down here with him. We stayed up there a couple days and one day there was a lot of noise in Ash Fork and everybody was yelling and they put some flags all over and Bill Pitts said there wasn't no more war. Bill Pitts and his wife jumped around and yelled and we were glad. Bill Pitts' wife cooked up a big meal and she came out there where me and Lemuel were at and she said, "Come on boys, we'll eat lots of somebody's goose." That's what she said. We had some beef but she said it was goose.

When I came back down here I helped my mother get some crops in and I stayed with my mother and so did my brother, Henry. My mother wasn't so strong no more and she didn't do very much. My sister, Susie, cooked for us and we had plenty of stuff to eat.

When it was winter, I went up to Drift Fence and I stayed up there with Jess Chick and his wife and he had some broncs up there and we broke those broncs all winter.

When it was spring I came down here and I told my mother, "I got to pay some money to that store up in Ash Rock. I'm going up there and work and I'm going to pay that money."

I asked my mother if she will be all right and if she's got lots of stuff. My mother said, "It's all right. I got lots of stuff and Susie cooks and I'll be all right. You pay that money in Ash Fork."

I went up to Bunk Groves and I stayed around there and I helped him cut some wood. I stayed there two months and when I got some money from cutting that wood I went to Ash Fork and I paid the money to the store.

After that I went and worked for a white man they called Daft Brown. I heard he maybe wanted some cowboys so I went over there and I worked for him. We took a whole lot of steers to Skull Valley over by Prescott. We stayed on that first night in the Chino Valley near King's place and then when it was the next day we took those cattle over to Skull Valley. I never been there before and it looked like a good place over there.

When it was the next morning they counted out some dry cows and some cows with calves and then in the next morning me and two white boys went back to Ash Fork and took the saddle horses and we loped all the way. I sure was tired. In the next day we got the rest of Daft Brown's steers and we drove them to Bill Pitts' place. Daft Brown was married with Bill Pitts' daughter. We stayed there by Gold Trap for one night and when it was the next day we drove those steers over to a canyon and we put them in a corral. In the next day we branded the young ones and we cut the nuts out of the ones if they were three years old and then we turned the rest of those horses loose.

Then I told Bill Pitts, "I'm going down there to Supai." He gave me my money and I came home down here. I told my cousin. I would break some horses for him and I rode those broncs around and I made them gentle. That's all I did.

I didn't stay down here very long and I got a letter from Daft Brown and he said I should come back up there to his place and work for him. I thought, "Maybe I'll stay down here", but I thought it would be good to get some more money so I went up

there. When I was coming up there I saw Bunk Grove near Gold
Trap and I helped him pick some beans for maybe three or four
days and then I went to Daft Brown's place. Lemuel Paya was
up there too and we put lots of steers on railroad cars and we
filled up fourteen of those cars.

When we were done Daft Brown told me he wants me to
work all winter up there. I said, "It's all right." I hauled
groceries and feed over there to the Chino Valley for those
cowboys and cattle over there. I hauled all that stuff in a wagon
with a good team. Sometimes when I started early I got down
there to Chino Valley when it was maybe eleven o'clock at
night. When those fellows heard me come in there they always
got up that cook and I had a lot of good food. When it was the
next day I always cut some wood for those fellows and I hauled
that wood in by the camp with that team. I was down there in
Chino Valley maybe two or three days, then I went back to Ash
Fork.

That road was always mud and there was lots of snow but I
had two teams on that wagon sometimes and I didn't get stuck. I
sure liked to work like that. I liked to ride in that wagon for a
long time. I never thought about nothing when I was driving
that wagon. I just kept going on and looking ahead of those
horses. I just liked to do that. I did that job all winter and I sure
liked it.

One time when I went back to Ash Fork it was night and I
ate and when I went out to the place where my bedding was, I
couldn't find that bedding so I went in and I told Daft Brown,
"Where's my bedding? I went out there where it was and it
wasn't there." He said, "Is it gone?" I told him, "It's not out
where it was." Daft Brown said, "We'll look around this place.
I lost lots of chickens and I think there are robbers around here."
We looked around and we saw some stuff by a fence. It was my
bedding, but two blankets and two new shirts and some pants

and some new boots were gone. I sure was sore and it was cold and I didn't have enough bedding so Daft Brown let me use some stuff.

When it was the next morning I went out and followed some foot marks for a long way but I couldn't go far and I didn't find nothing. In the next day I went to Chino Valley and Daft Brown told some police in Ash Fork and they looked around there and they said lots of stuff was getting robbed around that place.

When I came back from Chino Valley, I stayed one night with one of Daft Brown's cowboys on the way. After we all ate some Mexican came in by the camp and he was all beat up and he said, "I'm hungry. If you cook some food for me, I'll tell you where those robbers are at." Those cowboys said, "All right." They gave him some stuff to eat and he told them where those robbers are up in a cave near Daft Brown's place. All those cowboys went in Ash Fork and they got some police. I went over to Daft Brown's place and I loaded up that wagon with some stuff to take over there to Chino Valley. When I went by that camp when it was the next morning there was a lot of men with guns around there and they looked like soldiers but they didn't have no uniforms. They got those robbers up in that cave. There was three of them and they got them. They had a whole lot of stuff in that cave. Some fellow said, "It's like a store up in that cave." They robbed that stuff from all over. I got stuff back and I sure was glad of it. That Mexican was one of those robbers, but they beat him up and he told where they were at.

When I went on down to Chino Valley it snowed so much I got almost covered up on that wagon seat but I sure liked that snow when I was driving that wagon. It covered me all up and I was warm.

Supai Gathering at Drift Fence—Mark Learns to Trap

When it was April I took a load of stuff down to Chino Valley and there was a new boss in that camp and he didn't like me, and he told me to get out of that place. He said, "Indians are no good. I don't want no Indians around here." I didn't get my horse. I just went away and I walked over to Ash Fork. I walked for two days and I got to Daft Brown's place and I told him, "I want to quit. I'm not going to stay around here." I told Daft Brown about that white man down there and what he said. Daft Brown fired him and he got my horse for me but I didn't want to stay around there no more. I went away.

I went over to a place of a fellow they call Roy Wolf and I worked for him being a cowboy for maybe a month and I rounded up cattle for him. Then one day Coyote Jim came by that place and he told me my mother is sick. I quit that job and I went over by Ash Fork and I heard my brother was working over there. I went over there where he was and I told him, "My mother is sick and we better go down there to Supai." My brother said, "I like to keep this job and I don't want to quit. You go down there and if she's sick bad you come up here and tell me and I'll go down there."

I came down here and my mother's neck was sore inside and she was better. I stayed down here maybe two weeks and she was feeling better so I went up there to Roy Wolf's and I got some money from working there and I went to where my brother, Henry, was and he quit and he got some money and we bought a lot of groceries and brought all that stuff down here for my mother. She wasn't strong no more and her neck hurt so inside she couldn't work in the garden. I stayed down here maybe two weeks and I worked all the time in my mother's garden.

After a while I went up to where Thomas Yunosi was staying by Redlands ranch at the head of Cataract Canyon. My mother said she was all right so I went up there and I worked for a man at Redlands. I worked to make a wagon road up there with Thomas Yunosi. After a while that white man, Mr. Griffin, sent us over near Hubble Tank to cut some posts and that's what we did. Then we went back to Redlands and there was some other Supais there and we dug a pipeline and I'm boss because I can talk English good.

All those boys had to do their cooking and some didn't like to do that but I didn't care if I cook for myself. I liked to cook my food. Some of those boys were sore because they had to cook. They were sore because the ground got hard and they couldn't dig easy. And some of those boys wanted to quit. After a while all those Supais quit and I stayed there by myself. There was a Peach Dance down here and they quit and came back down here. I couldn't do all that work myself so I quit and I came down here too.

When I came in the canyon it was night and they were dancing. I danced in that circle dance for a little while and then

I came over here where my mother was and she was feeling better and Henry and Susie were taking care of her. I told my mother, "I'm going back up there by Redlands and I'm going to work up there." My mother said, "It's all right." I went back up there and some of those boys went back up there too. Dudley Manakadja and Fred Uqualla and Roger Toup went back up there too and we worked on that pipeline.

When we were up there two weeks, Fred Uqualla got sick in his stomach. He couldn't eat no stuff but water and he was hurting all the time. He told me, "Mark, I don't think I'll stay here long. I think I'll die in two days." I told one of those boys he should come down here and get Coyote Jim and Toby Uqualla. They are brothers of Fred Uqualla. We didn't sleep that night and we just stayed around and sat by Fred Uqualla. When it was the next day Coyote Jim and Toby Uqualla came up there and we just talked all day and all night. When it was the next morning before the sun was showing, he died.

After a while they put him in a blanket and put him on a horse and they took him over by the Hualapai Trail to bury him over there near where his father was buried too. I was behind those other fellows because I went to tell that white man we're going over by the Hualapai Trail. When I was riding along behind I could see where all that sickness had run out of Fred Uqualla's mouth and it was on the ground. It was all rotten blood and yellow sickness stuff. When I got up to where they were carrying him on that horse I saw all that stuff running out and, Jesus Christ, it smelled rotten.

When we buried him near the Hualapai Trail some Supais came up there from down here. When we took that blanket off his head it was all bloody. Jesus Christ, it looked like somebody smashed his head and that sickness was all over his head from his mouth and it smelled rotten. They just buried that blanket with him. Then we all came down here and lots of people cried and we had a funeral and we all cried.

After three days we went back up there to Redlands to work some more. Some of those other boys went back up there too and we got that pipeline put in all right and then it was November and it snowed all the time for a week and we didn't have no food in that place and we didn't have no wood. We went out in the snow and we got some wood and some rabbits and that's what we had. When I was getting some wood I saw where a wildcat had walked and I wanted to get his fur for gloves. I followed him around and I saw him in some cedar and I chased him and he climbed up in a tree. I had a pistol and I shot him in that tree and I took him back to the camp. I skinned him good and I hung that meat in a tree and I said, "My mother sure likes this meat." I thought I'd bring that meat down here for her to eat. Those other fellows said, "That's a good wildcat and you sure got him."

When it was the next day I came down here. I only got to Topacoba Hilltop in one day because the snow was deep. I came down here in the next day and there was some snow down here too.

My mother sure was glad to get that wildcat meat and she roasted it over a big fire. We all ate some of that meat and I said, "I better tan this skin." I soaked it in the river over night and I wrung it out and I tanned it with some deer brains I had dried in a sack from all those deer I got up there at Pine Springs and I hung it in my mother's house to save it.

My mother wasn't strong no more and she stayed down here all winter. I cut a lot of mesquite trees for her to burn to be warm. She stayed down here all winter and Susie stayed down here with her.

After two weeks I went up there to Drift Fence. There was lots of Supais up there in that winter and I stayed with Jess Chick and his wife, Lina, and Sinyella was up there too and he camped near us. There was plenty of people up there and there was a lot of wood and we could keep warm and I was glad of it. It was good to be with all those Supais. We all got along good and it was a happy time.

We cut lots of wood and when it didn't snow hard me and Jess Chick and Louis Sinyella and Flyn Watahomigie went out and we got wild horses. There was lots of studs around there and we got plenty of them. We built a corral from brush and we put those horses in there and we broke lots of them. We didn't have nothing to do but ride those broncs and we all liked to do that. Jess had a team up there and we made a tank around them so there'll be water for the horses in the summer maybe. All those men and boys worked on that tank and they rode those broncs all the time and the women cooked lots of stuff and they made baskets.

We made a sweat bath up there and lots of those boys took sweatbaths. There wasn't any water up there and we just rubbed ourselves off with some rags. I sure liked it up there in that camp. I wished my mother and Susie were up there too.

When it was almost spring, almost everybody around that camp got that flu sickness and some of those people almost died. I didn't get sick and just a few other people didn't get that sickness.

I came back down here when it was just beginning spring because I thought maybe my mother doesn't have no more firewood. When I got down here she still had lots of wood and she wasn't cold and I was glad because I was thinking about that up there in that camp. I helped my mother plant some corn and stuff and I stayed down here all summer and I worked in that garden and I broke some more horses for my cousin, Prince Wodo. Everybody had a good garden in that year and it was all right and there wasn't any sickness. I went up the Hualapai Trail

lots of times and I drove a lot of horses down in Hualapai
Canyon to Grapevine Spring and gave them water to drink
because there wasn't any water up there on top.

When it was September, I got a letter down here from Daft
Brown. He told me I should come up there and work for him
and haul some wood. I was down here all summer and I was
glad when I got that letter to come up there and work. When I
work down here I just work and that's all I do. When I work up
there I work and get some money too. I don't get no money
when I work down here.

I went up there to Daft Brown's and I worked up there for
him for three months. Daft Brown sold all his cattle and he
didn't have no money and he had to cut the wood he owned and
sell it and that's what I did.

When I didn't work there no more, I was coming down
here. I stayed up there at Hualapai Hilltop in a hogan Panameda
built. I was thinking about trapping so I stayed up there in that
hogan. There was another hogan up there too and an old Supai
man was living there. That was Kathada. He was the half-
brother of my mother and I went over there in his hogan and I
stayed with him because he was a relative. I came down here
and I got some corn and peaches and I took it back up there and
that's what we ate. I took some traps up there too and I set those
traps for coyotes so I could have that fur and sell it at Seligman
or Grand Canyon. I was thinking about it.

I put rabbit guts on those traps and I didn't cover them up
and the coyotes didn't get in those traps. There was a white
trapper camped a little way off and I went over there to that
camp and I asked him how I'm going to catch those coyotes. I
told him I'm using rabbit guts for bait and he said, "Rabbit guts
are no good." Then he gave me some good bait. He said it was
coyote shit. He said, "You go out and get coyote shit, and put a
lot of it in some water and boil it up good till its thick. Then you

can put it in a can or something and that stuff makes good bait."
He told me to set that trap near to a bush and bury it just a little in
some snow or dirt and put a little of that coyote shit on that bush.
When a coyote smells that stuff he'll come over there to piss on
the bush and he'll step in that trap.

I did what that white fellow said and I caught a coyote and
I went over there and told him and he said if I cut up that
coyote's bladder and kidney and some of his fat and boil it up
with the shit and keep it buried in the ground for a year that sure
makes good bait. He told me those coyotes can smell it for
maybe two miles and they'll come and get caught in a trap. I
made that bait like he told me and I never smelled anything so
bad.

I used that bait and I caught four coyotes, three foxes, four
wildcats, one badger and two skunks. I made up a lot of that bait
and I buried a gallon of it near the hogan.

I stayed up there till I caught all those animals and then I
came down here and I sent those skins to St. Louis. Somebody
said I'll get more money from that place. I sent all those furs
over there and I only got sixteen dollars and thirty-five cents for
all that stuff. I wanted some more, but that's all I got. I stayed
up there and set those traps all winter and I didn't get much more
stuff. I just stayed up there with that old man and I trapped. I
got wood and food for that old man too.

When I was still up in that hogan a white man they called
John Bishop came around there and he told me I should go over
to his place near Round Mountain and work for him. I went over
there and I cut some fence posts and I fixed some broken fence
and I put up some new fence too. I set in a lot of posts and some
Hualapai they called Jack Coho came over there and he helped
me but he said, "It's too hot," and he quit. Louis Sinyella, he
heard about that job when he was over there in Peach Springs
and he helped me put up some new fence for a few days and he

quit. He said, "I thought I was going to ride a horse over here. I don't want to just set these posts." Then he quit.

I tried to stretch some fence by myself but I couldn't do that alone. John Bishop told me I should come down here and get some boys to help so that's what I did. I asked some boys around here to come up there and work and help me and get some money. I asked a lot of those boys but they wouldn't go up there and work. They just wanted to stay down here all the time. I told those boys, "You're lazy, you boys. When I was young I worked all around and I did a lot of work. You don't want to go away from here and go away from these girls. You just want to be laying around with these girls all the time. You boys are lazy." They told me they didn't want to work. I said to those boys, "Do you want some money?" I showed them I had some money and they said, "Sure we want some of that money." I said, "Why don't you go out and work and get some money? Nobody gives you money when you only sit down here and you don't do nothing. Why don't you go out and work and get some money and you can buy lots of stuff? Those boys just said they don't want to work. My sister, Susie, was married with Kit Jones and she told me they're coming up there and maybe they'll bring some boys up there.

I went back up there to John Bishop's place and he asked did I get some help. I said, "No, I didn't get nobody." He said, "Why?", and I told him, "Those boys are lazy and they don't want to work." He asked me, "How do they get their grub and their bedding and stuff?" I told him, "I don't know how they're going to do it."

I kept working up there by myself and after a while Kit Jones came up and he had Mike Mooney with him and they helped me put up that fence and Susie cooked for us. After about three weeks we finished doing that and we got our money and went to the town and Susie got some groceries. John Bishop gave us some food too. We had a lot of stuff and we only had one pack horse and we didn't think that horse could bring all that stuff down here. John Bishop let us use a wagon and his team to bring that stuff to Hilltop. He was glad we got that fence done and he gave us a big sack of flour and some beef too and we went back to the town and I got some clothes with that money and I got a phonograph too. I still got that phonograph. I got some more flour for my mother too.

We brought all that stuff up there to Hualapai Hilltop and Kit Jones and Mike Mooney packed it down here. I took that wagon back to John Bishop and I rode over to Seligman. I just wanted to ride down there and I stayed at the Hualapais' camp over there. When I went over there those Hualapais said, Did you build that fence?" I said, "Yes, I got some Supais and got that fence built." I stayed at Seligman for two days and I just sat around and watched those Hualapais gamble. They always gamble. They said, "Mark, you come on and gamble and give us some of that money you got." I told them, "I got no money and I don't know how to gamble."

Then I went over to Peach Springs and I stayed with those two Hualapais, Doctor Tommy and Old Beecher. Those fellows are relatives and I learned how to hunt deer from them and I went over there to help them. I hunted some deer for them and I got two and I gave those two fellows all that meat and I kept those hides. They sure were glad to have that meat.

When I was there a week maybe that white man, Frank Cook, came over there and he said I should come over to his place and work for him and haul some water for steers and fix some fences. I kept hauling water for a month and then he told me I should come back when it's fall and help him round up some steers.

When I got through up there I came back down here and I helped my mother in her garden. My mother kept on working in that garden and I told her she's not strong enough to work all the time but she never stopped doing that when I told her to. She just kept on doing that just like Susie does. Susie don't do what I tell her.

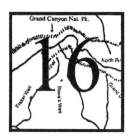

Trapping and Panning
Gold on the Colorado

When it was September, Frank Cook came down here to the canyon and he wanted me to go up on top with him and get some wild horses. I told my mother I'm going up there but she didn't want me to go but I said, "My brother and Susie will help you and take care of you."

When we went up by Frank Cook's we got lots of horses and I put shoes on some of those horses and when I was doing that a white man called Abe Kaufman came over there and he told Frank Cook he needed to have me work for him and Frank Cook said, "It's all right." Abe Kaufman said he wanted to have some cowboys. He said he came down here and I got Toby Uqualla and I asked a lot of boys to come up there and I asked Bela Wascogomie and he said, "I don't think I can go up there. I've got lots of work and I've got lots of horses to feed. I can't go up there." I couldn't get nobody else to go up there. That night Elmer Watahomigie came over where I was sleeping. He was a poor boy and didn't have nothing. He only had an old saddle and only a rope bridle. He didn't have no shoes and no hat and he had holes in his pants. He was poor because he was lazy. His father told him to work but the didn't work and he just laid around with the girls. That's what happens when you're lazy and lay around the girls. You get poor and you got no good saddle and no good clothes.

He said, "Have you enough boys?" I told him I couldn't get enough and he said he'd go up there and work and I was glad he said he'd go up there. When we got up there Abe Kaufman saw him and he said, "He's starving already. He's a poor boy and he must be lazy. If he's lazy here he gets fired." I said, "It's all right."

We got a whole lot of calves and dry cows and we put them in a pasture. We went over near Lagoon Lake and we got a lot of cattle there and we branded some calves and we cut out some more steers and dry cows and put them in another pasture on the other side of the lake. That was a big lake then. Every day when some cattle came to that lake we got them and cut out the dry cows and some steers. Elmer Watahomigie was working hard. He did good and I was glad.

We worked around that lake for maybe a week. Those cattle were wild like deer and we had it hard to catch them. When they smelled us they just ran off and got in some brush and it sure was hard to catch them.

After a while Abe Kaufman said, "I think I got enough cattle." We took those steers over to Seligman and it was cold. After we got those cattle to Seligman for selling them, it snowed for three days. We didn't see Abe Kaufman when we got over there. He had all those cattle and he was selling them and he was a rich man so he was around with those whores. There was lots of whores in Seligman. There was some white whores and some Chinese whores and some Mexican whores. Maybe there was some Indian whores over there too. That's where Abe Kaufman was. He went to see those whores.

It took maybe three or four days to get all those cattle weighed up and put in those cars. It was sure hard to do that and when we got done doing that, Abe Kaufman told us to take our saddles over to Rowe's Well and wait for him. Me and Toby and Elmer took those saddle horses over there and we waited there to get our money. When Abe Kaufman came over there he gave us our money and he said he don't need us no more. I got one hundred and sixty-four dollars. That sure was a lot of money and I went over to that Hualapai by Pine Springs and Elmer Watahomigie stayed up there too. Tony Uqualla came down here. Elmer bought a lot of stuff before he came down here. He bought some clothes and bedding and lots of stuff and he said he sure was glad he went up there and worked. He always worked good after that and he's not lazy and he wasn't a poor boy no more. I was glad that boy learned not to be lazy. I was glad he learned how to be a man.

When it was November, I came down here and it snowed all the time and I stayed up there in that hogan up at Hilltop and then the next day I came down here and I cut some wood for my mother and I rode around and saw some relatives and I was thinking about trapping. I went up there to Hualapai Hilltop and I stayed there by myself. I dug up that bait I buried up there. Jesus Christ, when I smelled it, it sure was strong. I put that bait on some bushes with a little stick and I set those traps around those bushes.

One day the agent came up there to where I was and he said I should cut a pine tree and pack it down here for the Christmas time. Everybody was glad to go to Christmas. We went up to the schoolhouse and the agent told us to wait for Santa Claus and after a while he came in the school with red clothes on and a long beard and he gave us candy and stuff and it was Thomas Yunosi who was Santa Claus. The government gave us a lot of stuff. I got two sacks of tobacco and some socks and a handkerchief. That's all I got.

When we were through with Christmas the agent said we will have a big feast on the next day and everybody's going to eat a lot. Everybody brought lots of food and the government gave us some meat and we boiled it all up and everybody ate a lot.

On the next day I went back up to that hogan by myself and I was sure glad I was alone. I trapped maybe twelve more coyotes and eight more wildcats and two badgers. I made lots more bait out of all that shit and fat and stuff and I buried it and I was thinking about trapping in the next winter.

After a while I got some more coyotes and wildcats and badgers and I brought all those furs down here and I sent all that stuff to St. Louis and I went back up there and I tried to trap some more furs and I took some corn and coffee and some stuff with me that I got from the mail from Grand Canyon. I got some rabbits for eating up there too and that's what I ate.

I didn't get no more coyotes up there but I got three grey foxes and five more wildcats and when it was February and I sent some more furs to St. Louis. I got a check from those fellows for the first bunch of furs I sent and I only got twenty-two dollars for all that stuff. I brought some of that wildcat meat down here for my mother and Susie and Henry and they sure were glad of it. I brought some rabbits down here too and my mother said, "You save all those rabbit skins and you bring them down here and I can make a blanket."

I went back up there to Hilltop and I stayed there till it was April and I didn't get nothing but rabbits and then I came down here to put in some early corn. I put two of my fields in early corn. My mother helped me plant that corn and she worked slow and I was wishing she didn't work in the field but she wanted to do that. I watered my horses from Hilltop down at Grapevine Spring. I told some of these fellows down here, "We should make a cement tank up there to water those horses." Those boys wouldn't do nothing. They all wanted to stay down here all the time and be with the girls. That's just like they do now. Lots of those fellows got horses up there but they wouldn't go up there and build a cement tank so those horses could have some water.

Supai Jack and some other fellows said they'd help and we got some cement from the agent and we put in that cement tank. There was a spring near that tank and after a few days it was filled up and those horses had some water to drink. I drove some horses over to that tank so they'd know there was some water in there. Supai Jack and some other fellows had some cattle up there and they had some water now too.

When we got through working up there I came back down here and I worked in my garden and I helped my mother and Susie pack some peaches in the storage houses up there on the cliff. When fall came I went up there to that hogan at the top of the Hualapai Trail and I stayed there alone and I trapped some more and looked after my horses. Some white men poisoned all those coyotes up there and I didn't trap any. They were all dead and the foxes and wildcats were all gone too and I didn't get none. I just stayed up there and looked after my horses and I just came down here and got some cornmeal from my mother and I hunted some rabbits and that's what I ate. I liked to be up there by myself and I was never afraid when it was night. I heard some owls but I wasn't sacred.

When the snow came it was cold and I liked to be in that hogan with that stove and it was warm in there. When I got where I didn't have no food I came down here and I got some cornmeal and some dried peaches and I went back up there the next day. I had lots of stuff to do. I had to chop lots of wood and melt some snow and look after those horses and I never got lazy. I sure liked it up there. I liked to sit next to the stove and think about what I am doing and what I did do and all the things and stuff I have seen.

Nobody came up there to visit me and one day I went over where that white trapper was camped but he wasn't there so I didn't see nobody. I put out a lot of traps but I didn't get nothing. One day I went around and I looked at all of those traps and one was gone. I looked all around where I put that trap and I found it and it was shut and there was only some mountain lion claws in that trap. I took those claws out and the next day I came down here to get some cornmeal and dried peaches and dried pumpkin and I brought those claws down here and I showed them to my mother and Susie and Kit Jones and they all laughed and they said, "Why didn't you get all that mountain lion? He only left his claws for you." They laughed and I laughed too.

When it was spring I came down here and I didn't have no fur. I told my mother, "I'm going to Pine Springs and visit my relative, Doctor Tommy." He wanted me to come up there and get some deer for him. My mother said, "It's all right." Don't stay up there a long time so you can help with the crops." I went up there and I camped at Hilltop the first night and then I went over to Pine Springs. I didn't find Doctor Tommy and I asked Frank Beecher's uncle where he was at and he said he was over by Blue Mountain, the other side of Pine Springs. When it was the next day I went over there and I found Doctor Tommy. I stayed there for a while and a white man came over there and he asked if some Hualapais could wrangle some horses for him. He had a ranch near the railroad. Those Hualapais said, "We don't want to go." I told him, "I'll go over there."

I left my horse at that Hualapai camp and I went over there to that white man's ranch in his car with him. They called him Henry Bacon. He had some Hualapais over there too. His horses were near Hackberry and his foreman was called Tye Reed and he told me I can wrangle when it's day and a white boy was wrangling when it was night. I was glad because I was afraid if I wrangle when it's night maybe I'll fall asleep and I'll lose those horses.

I stayed with those horses maybe three weeks and then Tye Reed told me I should go over by Freeze Wash and wrangle some more horses. I told one of those Hualapais, I don't know that place over there and I think I'll go home." Tye Reed told me I could take some horses over to a place they call Sandy. I said, "I don't know that place." He told me there's only one way and I won't get lost and I can get ten dollars for every day. Those Hualapais told me I should go and get that money. I told him, "I'll take those horses down there to that place."

The first night I got to Cedar Ranch and I put those horses in a pasture there. When it was the next day I took them south and I thought I got lost and I didn't see nobody and I didn't know that country. I knew there was Hualapais near that place they call Sandy but I didn't see no Hualapais and I thought I was lost. When the sun was down I saw some white cowboys and they told me how to go and I was only two miles from that place. When I got there I put those horses in a pasture and I got some food and that white man there gave me a cigar and he told me to sleep in a bed in his house. He said there's so many rattlesnakes and it's bad to sleep on the ground around there. It was hot and there was a ditch with some water in it and that's where I took a bath. I just got in that water and I got cool. It was three days to get those horses over there and I got thirty dollars and I sure was glad. I rode back to that ranch in a car with Mr. Bacon and then I went to Peach Springs.

When I went there one of those Hualapais had a letter that somebody sent up there for me and they said my relative, Dudley Manakadja is sick and you come down here in Supai and see him. I went to Pine Springs with one of those Hualapais and I got my horse and I came down here.

When I came down here he was better. I watered my fields and I plowed and I put in some crops and I just stayed down here all summer. In that summer we had a big storm and all the irrigation ditches broke and we had a lot of work to fix them. I watered my horses too and I got the crops picked and we stored a lot of peaches.

When it was fall, I went up there to Rowe's Well and I worked up there with George Yumatiska and Toby Uqualla and Supai Jack. After a while Roger Toup came up there too. We cut lots of wood to run a pump. We did that work for a fellow they called Al Sanford. He paid us good and we got lots of wood and some food too. We camped by Rowe's Well and we stayed right there. We hunted for some deer too but we didn't get any. I guess some white men got all those deer.

When it was still January we got done cutting that wood up there and we had the money and we went to Seligman and I bought a lot of groceries and I brought a lot of that stuff down here. When I came down here I heard there was some jobs up there at Grand Canyon. Me and Joseph Watahomigie and Roger Toup went up there and they told us they wanted some stones and tar for a place to walk by the canyon for those tourists. Bela Wescogomie came up there too and we put those places to walk around there. When we got that done we dug some places around up there and it was all mud all the time and I was climbing a ladder and my leg got swelled up so I quit.

I went where we were camping and I made a sweatbath and I went in there every day for a week and my leg was better. I wanted to have that job back but I couldn't get it. Some white man around there said he'd give me three dollars a day if I panned gold for him down on the Colorado River. I told him, "I don't know how to pan gold." He showed me how I can scrape that gravel in a pan and wash it around and wash off the black sand and, Jesus Christ, there was gold in there. Sometimes it was just like the sand and sometimes it was big. When I got that gold I put it in a can. I worked down there by myself and he couldn't get nobody else down there.

One day he got a white boy to work down there but he didn't do nothing for a week and when that fellow came down here, I said, "That white boy doesn't help me. He only sleeps all the time." The boss ran him off. When he went he took two cans of that gold with him. I don't think nobody ever caught him. Maybe he's rich now.

I just worked on that gravel by myself. Louis Sinyella and his brother worked down there in Indian Gardens and they were cleaning up an old mine. One night they came down there to the river where I was and they told me, "You know how to do this now and sometime we'll come down here and get that gold. You know how to get that gold now and that's what we'll do." I said, "We don't own this place no more and we don't have nobody say we can come down here and get gold. We have to ask those white men now or maybe we'll get in trouble. They said they were just making a joke and we all laughed and we ate some food.

After a while I couldn't get no more gold and that white fellow told me I can quit. I quit looking for that gold when it was the last day of September and I got one hundred and ten dollars. Then I went up there by Indian Gardens and I worked with Louis Sinyella and his brother. I worked there a month and then we packed our stuff up to Grand Canyon and we got some money. There was lots of white people all around there and they were looking at the canyon. They came up there every day in those cars and on that train and they just keep coming.

When we got our money I had almost three hundred dollars and I sure felt good to have all that money. I went over there near Rowe's Well and Kit Jones and Susie were over there and I helped him work over there. We cleaned off a lot of land. We cleaned off maybe four acres. A white man they called Emery Kolb told us to do that. He said his brother is bringing an airplane up there and that's where they're going to put it. We cleared off all that land and Kit Jones got some money for that and he didn't give me any. He borrowed two hundred and fifty dollars from me and he said, "I'm going to buy a good car." He got that car from a fellow and they called it a Ford. I never got that money back from him. I asked him about it lots of times and I never got that money back.

Doc Pardee's Wild West Show

After I left the Colorado I started to come down here and I went to Drift Fence for the first night and Watahomigie was there and he said, "Why are you going down there to Supai?" I told him, "My mother is down there and maybe she needs some wood or some food or some stuff. I'm going down there to help her." He said, "She's all right and she's got lots of help down there. Why don't you stay up here with me and help me get wood and hunt some rabbits to eat?" He was an old man and he only had his wife up there and I thought maybe he was too old to do all that stuff. I stayed up there with him.

There wasn't much snow in that winter. There was lots of rabbits. I just stayed up there all winter and nothing happened. Watahomigie told me lots of things he did when he was young and he told me some of those funny things and we all laughed. He told me I can't hunt rabbits. He said, "Only the old Indians know how to get those rabbits," and I told him, "I can get some rabbits too." I took his pistol and there was only five bullets in it and I went out and when it was just a little while I went back there and I had five rabbits. Watahomigie laughed and he said, "I guess you can get those rabbits all right." I never shot so good before. He only told me I couldn't get those rabbits so I'll go out and get a lot of them.

When it was spring, I came down here and I planted my early corn and I helped my mother too. I rode some broncs too and I still could break them good. I don't like nobody to break my colts. I always broke those colts myself. I ride them a while and I cut their nuts out and I ride them till they're not sick no more. I just did all that by myself. I only went with some other fellows when they are riding broncs. Those fellows had one horse up there by that rodeo place and he threw everybody off him. They said I should ride that horse and I just said, "No, I won't ride that horse." One time I went up there when they had that horse up there and I rode that horse and I didn't get bucked off. I just rode him till he stopped and then I got off and I just walked away and all those boys were yelling and hollering and I was sore because I knew they wanted me to get thrown off and maybe get into some wire. I didn't do it. I just rode that horse till he stopped and I went up there and I rode him the next day too and they all yelled and hollered but I didn't get thrown off.

When it was fall I went up there by Hualapai Hilltop and I trapped up there. I didn't get nothing. When it was February, I still didn't get no coyote. I quit trapping up there and I came back down here and Foster Marshall was down here. He told me a white man they called Doc Pardee was over by Phoenix and he was going to get up a rodeo and he said, "Why don't you come over there and we'll be in that rodeo and we'll get some money?" He said we were going to ride and rope and bulldog and dance and sing if we go over there. I told him, "I guess I'll go over there." Ralph Rogers and Mack Putesoy and James Wescogomie and Louis Sinyella and Dean Sinyella and Supai Mary went over there too. We got some tickets for the train up there at Grand Canyon from Doc Pardee and we went over there to Phoenix on that train.

When we got over there to that place it was in the night and Doc Pardee put us in a cabin till it was morning. When it was the next day we went in the town and he told us to put some tipi tents up around there. We put up those tents and we put some fireplaces around there and we hung up a whole lot of pots and jars and stuff Doc Pardee gave us. He told us, "Don't cook on those pots and jars. You just sit here and look like Indians so people can see you." Supai Mary just sat in that place and she made some baskets and those people looked at her. All those people they just came around and they looked at us and we didn't like it when they did that but Doc Pardee gave us money for doing that so we did it. I don't know why they wanted to look at us. There's Indians everyplace and they can see them and they don't have to pay nothing. I thought maybe they wanted to see Supais and we are different. I don't know why. Sometimes some of those people threw some pennies in there and Supai Mary said, "Thanks". I never said that. I didn't say nothing. One day Doc Pardee put a Hopi in there with us too and he made a lot of headdresses out of turkey feathers and we wore those headdresses. I sure liked that headdress I wore.

After a while there was a show every day when it was afternoon. James Wescogomie and Foster Marshall rode broncs. They did that every day and they didn't get thrown off. There was a Maricopa boy there too and he did the bulldogging. They called him Louis Sundice and we liked him. He was a good fellow. We got sixty dollars every month and we sure were glad to get all that money. We were in a parade sometimes too. We walked all around that place and sometimes they rode us around in a truck and we wore those headdresses.

When it was February we all moved up to that mesa south of Phoenix and when we moved over there Doc Pardee got some

Pima boys and they played a band and they rode on horses. There was a show and a parade every day. The Hopis always danced but we didn't dance. The Hopis always danced. We all had those headdresses. I sure wish I had that headdress now.

Sometimes it rained and those tipi tents don't keep out no water and we got wet and my bed was in water sometimes. I think we didn't build those tents right. We just made those tipi tents like Doc Pardee told us.

Doc Pardee had a white horse and he called him White Angel. Jesus Christ, he sure was a bronc. When that Maricopa boy said he wanted to ride those other broncs in that show with us Supais, Doc Pardee told him, if he can ride that White Angel he can ride those broncs in the show so he rode that horse one time and he got thrown off after four jumps and that bronc stepped on him and broke him somewhere in his chest. Doc Pardee took him away someplace and we didn't see that boy after that. We sure liked that boy.

There was lots of white people and they always came over to that show and Doc Pardee got three dollars from them when they came over there to see that show. He sure got a lot of money.

One day me and a Mexican boy they called Yaki, rode a race on horses and we had to jump over some fences they put up. I never was on a horse when he jumped over a fence and it was hard for me and I nearly fell off. Then those other Supais put on some Indian britches and those headdresses and they got on some paint horses bareback and they rode around the circle and those Supais were supposed to jump over those fences with those paint horses and they never jumped over fences before and they all fell off and hung on to those horses necks and everybody laughed and Doc Pardee laughed and he said, "It's a show, so it's all right."

One day I was watching that Hopi make some headdresses and Doc Pardee came over there and he said, "All those Supai

boys want to go home. They want to quit and go home." He
asked me if I'm going to quit and I said, "I don't know if I'm
going to quit," I told him, "If one more Supai stays up here
maybe I'll stay up here."

I talked with those boys and Dean Sinyella said, "I'm
getting lots to eat up here and I'm going to stay." I told Doc
Pardee, "I'm going to stay and so is Dean Sinyella." I told him,
"We're getting lots of food up here and we're getting money and
if we go back home down there, there's nothing." Louis Sinyella
said after that he'll stay but Doc Pardee told him, "You bought
so much stuff and you owe money to me too. You spend so
much money and you owe me four dollars so you can't stay.
You go home. Don't stay around here." Louis Sinyella sure was
sore and he didn't pay that money. He just went off and just me
and Dean Sinyella stayed up there and so did all those Hopis and
those other Indians.

After two weeks we all moved again to another place near
Phoenix and we put up those tipi tents again, and we had a big
one and we kept our horses in there too. There was one of those
shows every day and we always rode.

After two weeks we all moved again to another place near
Phoenix and we put up those tipi tents again, and we had a big
one and we kept our horses in there too. There was one of those
shows every day and we always rode.

One day a big white man came around for that show. He
was big but he was short and his woman was tall. He took a big
anvil that weighted five hundred pounds maybe and he had a
piece of leather around that anvil and he picked that up with his
teeth, and he just stood there and held that anvil with his teeth.
Jesus Christ, he was a strong man. He said, "Who weighs two
hundred pounds?" Doc Pardee said, "I weigh two hundred
pounds." That strong fellow picked up that anvil with his teeth
and then Doc Pardee climbed up on that anvil and he stood on it.

Jesus Christ, I never saw nothing like that. That fellow never even moved a little and he just stood there and Doc Pardee stood on that anvil. Then that fellow put a potato on his wife's neck when she bent over and then he picked up an axe and he chopped on her neck and the potato just fell off on both sides, cut in half. He never even cut that woman. Jesus Christ, I never saw nothing like that before. I thought he was going to chop off that woman's head and he didn't even cut her. He went away with that woman on that same day and he never came back there.

When it was March some show came across that bridge to Phoenix and I saw it. They had some camels and a baby camel and we saw them. I never saw a camel before, and they had some little paint horses too. When it was the next day, Doc Pardee told us to take all those tents down and we did that, and it took us all the day for it. When it was night he paid those Pima boys and those Papagos and Navajos and Hopis. He didn't pay me and Dean Sinyella. He told us to pack all that stuff away in a place in Phoenix and then he paid us. Then he took us in a car to the train station and we got on a train and we went to Grand Canyon. I was sorry to go back there. I wished I was staying at Phoenix where it was a warm place and we got lots of stuff to eat. I was sorry to go away from there and Dean Sinyella said he was sorry to go too. We liked to be in that show.

Hopi Snake Dance

We stayed up there in Grand Canyon for three days and I bought some groceries up there at Babbitts and I mailed all that stuff to Supai and then I came home down here. It was April in 1928.

My mother sure was glad of it when I came down here. She thought maybe somebody would kill me when I was up there in Phoenix. She told me she cried a lot about that when I was up there. I helped my mother put in some crops and I thought my mother looked old and I told her she shouldn't work hard in that garden. I don't know how old she was but she looked old and I told her not to work hard but she kept doing it.

I had a lot of buckskins down there I didn't tan yet and I was tanning all those buckskins. I got a letter from one of those Hopi boys I knew up there at Second Mesa and he told me why don't I go up there to that Hopi Snake Dance when it was August. I thought, "I'll go up there to that dance." I had five buckskins and I worked on those hides and I got them all tanned and I thought, "I'll take those buckskins up there to those Hopis and I'll get some stuff when I trade them." I had to put some shoes on two horses because that was a long way to ride up there. I told my mother, "I'm going to go up there to that Hopi Snake Dance. I got a friend up there and I'm going up there and visit him and see that Snake Dance." My mother said, "Are you going up there by yourself?" I told her I was going alone and she said, "You be careful of those Navajos. They might kill you and rob you to get your stuff." I asked some boys if they are going up to that Snake Dance, but nobody said he's going so I went up there alone.

When it was the twenty-third of August I started to go up there. When it was the first night I camped at Rowe's Well. There was some Supais up there but I camped by myself and I ate some food and I went to sleep. When it was the next day I got to Cameron Bridge by the Little Colorado River. It was cloudy that day and it made it good because it was cool. There was a store at that place and I bought some hay and I fed those two horses. There was a lot of Navajos around that store and they talked to me but I don't understand what they say.

When it was early in the next morning, I went to go to Tuba City. I got to that place when it was about noon and there was a Hopi there and he was a friend of the Supais and I stayed there with him. He said, "Mark, do you bring anybody with you?" I told him I was just by myself and he said, "Why don't you bring some boys with you? If some Navajo boys see you alone, maybe they'll think you're a rich man or something and they'll kill you maybe." He said, "I'm going up there to that Snake Dance tomorrow with a wagon and you go over there with me." I sure was glad he was going up there because I didn't like to think about those Navajo boys and how they might kill me.

When it was the next morning we went off in his wagon. He had a lot of fruit and chili and stuff to sell at the Snake

Dance. I had a good breakfast his woman made for me before we went and I sure felt good. I just tied my horses on the back of his wagon and I rode along with him in his wagon. We talked to each other in English good. He went to that school in Keams Canyon. I never went up there to that Snake Dance before and I didn't know that road very good but he showed me some places to go with my horses so I can get there quicker ahead of him so I went that way and he kept going on that wagon road. It sure was hot.

When it was night I got to a place where some Hopis lived and I stayed there. I knew those Hopis when they used to come down here in Supai and trade and I gave that Hopi man one of those buckskins and he said, "When you come back you stop here and I'll give you something." I said, "It's all right." On the next day I went over to Second Mesa and I was there when it was noon and my friend was there. He was sitting on a roof watching the road and he saw me and when I got there he just jumped down and he ran up and he was sure glad and so was I and we laughed and his wife was glad too. I stayed at his house but I didn't sleep in the house because he told me that house was full of bedbugs. I just slept on the roof and I never got no bedbugs on me.

When it was early the next morning he woke me up and he said, "Get up! Get up! We're going to see a long race." When I came down that ladder his wife came out there and she said, "Come in this house and take your hat off and your shirt off. I'm going to wash you." I did what she told me to do and there was a big tub of soapweeds in some water in there and I went over there and took a lot of that stuff and I was going to put it on my head but she came over and she knocked it off my hands and she said, "No, you're not going to do this. I'm going to wash your head and then you don't have to worry about the snakes." Then she washed my head off and I laughed when she was doing that.

I put my clothes on and I went out and sat on a big rock to watch that race. After a while I saw those men running a long way off. Maybe there was thirty of them and they had bells on and they were running up a hill and one fellow was ahead and all of them were hollering. Everybody was hollering. I asked my friend why they were hollering and he said, "They're hollering so it will make them keep running." When they stopped running some of those fellows took off their clothes and they put paint on them. Then they grabbed some corn and they ran around and some little boys painted white ran away with some corn and some girls chased them all around. Navajo girls chased them too and everybody ran around and hollered. Then we went back to my friend's house and we ate some food and then we went to his garden and we got some corn. We did that all day.

When it was about four o'clock they practiced the Snake Dance and I asked my friend, "How do they pick up those snakes?", and he told me, "They do that with their bare hands." I said, "I think they pulled the teeth off those snakes and they don't bite with teeth." My friend told me, "If you say that to a Snake Man, sometimes they'll pull off your clothes and tie you down where those snakes are and you can see if they got teeth and probably they'll kill you if they bit you. That's what happens if you say that to a Snake Man." When my friend told me that, I never said that no more.

When they practiced that Snake Dance they used some little corn tassels for snakes and they sang real low songs and they shook small rattles.

When it was early in the morning they woke me up and my friend's wife washed me again and we watched that long race. Lots of kinds of Indians were there. When we were going to that race we saw a Hopi woman. They called her Nell and she sold the biggest basket I ever saw for a thousand dollars. She got that money easy and I sure wished I had a basket like that to sell. It was so big four men could get in it and it had lots of kinds of designs on it. A man who was working on that Santa Fe railroad bought that basket. He gave her a thousand dollars and I saw that money when he gave it to her. I never saw so much money before.

When we went to see the Snake Dance, my friend told me those Snake Men don't have nothing to eat all day. Those other men they called them Antelope, they can eat some stuff if they want to. We just ate stuff all day. Every place we went somebody said, "Let's go eat." I ate maybe forty times in that day. All day when I'm eating and walking around I was wondering how they're going to pick up those snakes. I asked my friend, "Do they rattle?" He told me, "Yes."

When it was night we went up there to see that dance. Those Antelopes came out and they walked around a little cottonwood hogan. They just walked around it slow about four times and they had white paint on them. After a while those Snake Men came and they were red all over. They had a bow and arrow and lots of red feathers. They walked fast and they went around like soldiers. They just sang low for a long time. My friend told me, "They're ready now." I sure was scared. Those fellows put those snakes in their mouths and they held on to them in their hands and, Jesus Christ, they sure rattled and rattled and rattled and I didn't see them bite those fellows. They just walked around and some of the Antelopes held on to bull snakes but those Snake Men had those rattlesnakes. They walked around with those snakes and they waved feathers at them and I sure was scared. I thought, "Maybe they'll all get killed." Nobody got bit.

When they got through those Snake Men made some circles and two of them picked up all those snakes and they threw them in that circle. Then all the Snake Men picked up all the snakes and they ran off with them and they let them go someplace. I was wishing they'd kill all those snakes. My friend told me, "When you're going around here and you're looking for your horses and you see some snakes, don't kill those snakes. If you kill a snake maybe the Snake Men will make a snake from you." I told him, "I won't kill no snakes."

When it was the next day I told my friend, "I'm going home." His wife told me, "No, you're not going home. You're going to help in the garden and then you can go home the next day." I worked in that garden for all the next day and I told my friend, "I'm going home tomorrow." He told me, "I'll give you three blankets and three saddle blankets." I told him, "I'll give you four buckskins." That's what we did and the next day I started to come home. I went back to that other Hopi's place about noontime and I stayed there. They told me to come again the next year and I said, "I'll come if I got any buckskins." That Hopi gave me three saddle blankets for that buckskin I gave him.

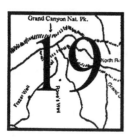

Another Indian
Murdered by White Men

When I was ready to start to go home from the Snake Dance two Hopi boys told me, "Why don't you go over there to Moenkipi to see the Butterfly Dance some Hopis are going to do over there? Why don't you go over there with us?" I said, "I'll go over there."

When it was that night we got over there to Moenkopi and when it was early in the next morning I saw that dance. I thought that was a good dance and I liked it and everybody was dressed up. Those people danced all day. That dance looked like it was good for exercise. Those Hopis do lots of dances and I sure liked to see them. I was wishing I could do some of those dances. Those Hopi boys said, "Let's go up there where those Piutes live and see some of those Piute girls up there. We never been up there and you go up there with us." I said, "Maybe my horses will be too tired if I go up there, so I won't go up there." They said, "It's all right."

I rested my horses and when it was the next day I started to go home. I didn't see nobody when I was going along. No

Navajo and nobody else and I was glad. I don't like to be where lots of people are for very long. I like to be alone sometimes. When it was that night I got to Coconino Basin and I stopped maybe two miles from a little store over there and I got some bread and some meat and I ate that stuff and then on the next day I got to Rowe's Well and I camped there by myself and I didn't visit any of those Supais over there.

The next day I came home down here. I told a lot of those boys and I told my mother about that Snake Dance. I told them all about what I saw up there. My mother said, "Some old people told me those Hopis always do that Snake Dance." I told her, "I think they pull the teeth off. They must have somebody who pulls off those teeth." My mother said, "I don't know if they do." I wasn't afraid to say that. I just said, "Maybe they pull the teeth out."

I gave one of those blankets I got to my mother and I gave her a saddle blanket too. I gave two saddle blankets to Susie too and I kept that other stuff. I put that stuff away. I just used one of those saddle blankets. It had red on it.

One day I got a letter from the Hualapai, Frank Wilder, and he told me I should come up there to Rowe's Well and help him build a fence up there. I told my mother I'm going up there and she said it was all right. When I went up there Dean Sinyella was up there too and we cut posts for that fence.

One day frank Wilder wanted me to go to Seligman with him in a car and I told him, "I don't want to go in there because I'm supposed to be working over here." He told me it was the same as working and we'll get paid for it because we were going to get some groceries. We went in there to Seligman and we got some groceries and Frank Wilder wanted to stay around that place for a while and I didn't want to stay there. He was sore about that. When we were going back we saw some cars on the road and there was some Mexicans there and Frank said, "I'm going to stop and see if they got some trouble." They didn't have no gas in that car and Frank gave them some. He didn't give them a lot and they said, "You come back there to Seligman with us or maybe we'll run out of gas again and we'll be stuck." I told Frank, "Don't go back there with those fellows. It's going to be dark and we got to go back there where we're camping." He said, "I'm going back there with those fellows," and we went back there with them. When we were coming into the town I saw a car with some police in it and it was behind us. I told Frank Wilder, "If you stop for that gas those police are going to make us get some trouble."

When he stopped that car in that gas station, one of those police got out and he came over by us and he said, "Are you drunk?" and we told him, "No, we're not drunk." We didn't have nothing to drink, but he said, "I think you are drunk." Then he took the rifle out of that car. It was broke and we didn't have no bullets but he took it out of there. Then he told me to get out of that car and he got in there and he drove that car away and Frank Wilder was still in there.

I didn't know where they went so I just stayed there by that gas station and I thought, "Maybe they'll come back here." When it was dark they didn't come back and I just stayed there. When it was the next morning I wanted to get some food and I was looking for some place where I can eat. I saw that white man we were fixing that fence for and he told me, "Do you know about Frank Wilder?" I told him, "I'm waiting for him so we can go back there and fix that fence." That white man said, "He's dead." I asked that fellow what he was dead for and he told me, "The policeman shot him last night because he was drunk and he had a gun and he tried to run off." I told that fellow, "We didn't have nothing to drink and that gun was broke and we didn't have no bullets." He told me they had a meeting about it and he said they said that policeman was all right because Frank Wilder was drunk and he had a gun."

I told that white man, "I want to go back there to Rowe's Well and get my stuff and my horse and I'm going home." I was kind of afraid to be near all those white men. They all said it was all right when that policeman shot Frank Wilder dead and he wasn't drunk and that gun was broke. That fellow told me I'll have to find some way to get over there to Rowe's Well by myself.

After a while, I got on a truck some Hualapai was taking over there and I got over there to Rowe's Well and I got my stuff and my horse and I was coming down here. When I got up there to Hilltop, Dean Sinyella and Louis Sinyella were up there and they heard about what happened and they wanted me to go over there to Frank Wilder's funeral by Peach Springs. I went over there to Peach Springs with those fellows and those Hualapais asked me how we were drunk and I said, "We didn't have no wine and no whiskey." Some of those Hualapais said, "When they had that meeting about that over there in Seligman, that policeman said he found some wine in that car and half of it was gone." I said, "We didn't have no wine and I think that police-man put that wine in there. We didn't have no wine. We weren't drunk."

All those Hualapais were pretty sore and I was sore too. We found out they called that policeman Bob Jones and some of those Hualapais said maybe they'll get that fellow and do some-thing. Maybe that Bob Jones heard about that because he went off someplace. Some white doctor over at Kingman came over there and he cut open Frank Wilder's body and I guess he looked around in there and he said Frank Wilder didn't have nothing to drink. They didn't do nothing to that policeman and those Hualapais didn't do nothing to him and he went away.

When they were having that funeral those Hualapais talked about that all night and they said maybe they're going to get a lawyer and they'll get that policeman. One of those Hualapais said, "If we get a lawyer he will be a white man. There aren't no Indian lawyers. We can't trust a white man if we try to get the law on a white man." I came back down here and I helped my mother and then I went up there to that hogan on the Hualapai trail to trap some more, but I didn't get much. All those animals are gone. They were dead or something. There was snow all the time in that winter and it got deep way up.

When it was January, I went over there to Pine Springs and I stayed over there for a while and I helped some fellow trap. I took my traps over there and I trapped with him and I got two foxes and five wildcats. Then I heard Frank Wilder's wife got another man already and those Hualapais said they aren't going to get a lawyer, to get that policeman. They just said, "It's all over."

When it was spring I heard my bother, Henry, got pneumonia over by Grand Canyon and I came home down here and I asked that fellow who was taking the mail how my brother is and he said he was all right. My mother cried all the time about that but my brother got better so I just stayed down here and worked in the garden and I took care of my horses. I had fourteen horses but I didn't have no cattle.

I just stayed down here all summer and I just kept working on. I got some hides and I was thinking maybe I'll go to that Snake Dance again. I got all those hides tanned and my garden was good. I wrote a letter to my friend up there by Second Mesa and I asked him when is that Snake Dance going to be and he said it was going to be on the twenty-eighth of August and I thought maybe it was too late already so I didn't go up there.

Cheated Again by the Fur Company—Another Hopi Snake Dance— Carrying the Mail and Freezing the Feet

When it was fall time I took a lot of food up there to Hualapai Hilltop and I just stayed up there and trapped and looked after my horses. I had a whole lot of that bait and I used it on those traps. I got five coyotes and three foxes and I got some wildcats too and I brought that meat down here for my mother. My mother said she'd sure like to have a porcupine to eat too, but I never got any. I set some traps down there by Navajo Falls and I put some figs on those traps and I got some of those raccoons. They sure liked those figs and I got those fellows in those traps. My brother looked after those traps for me when I was up there at Hualapai Hilltop.

I sent all those hides to that St. Louis place again and when I got a check from that place I only got twelve dollars. I sent that money back to that place and I told them I want those hides back. They said they already sold those hides and I got that money back. I didn't want that check and my sister, Susie, said,

"You put your name on that check and I'll take it." That's what I did I put my name on it and I gave it to my sister.

I went back up there to that hogan but I didn't trap no more. I just took care of my horses. I liked to stay up there when its winter. I don't like to stay down here and eat coffee and bread. I like to eat meat so I just stayed up there and I ate lots of rabbits.

One day I walked in that snow all day and I got wet all over and I took my clothes off and I went in the hogan and I got dry and I sure was hot and I thought maybe some sickness was in me. I just laid in that hogan for three days and I thought I'm getting worse so I got out of there and I saddled a horse and I came down here. The wind was hard all the way down here and I couldn't see good and my eyes were full of water and I coughed all the way down here. I tied my face in a handkerchief and then I didn't cough so much. I went to where the agent was and he gave me some pills and some grease to rub on me and then I just stayed with my mother and she had a fire in her hogan and she made me warm and I sure felt better. My mother got some stones hot and then she tied them up in some rags and she put them on my chest all the time and I got better.

Then I told my mother, "I'm going back up there to Hilltop and see about my horses. She said, "You go up there and see about those horses and then come back down here." I said, "I guess I'll do that." I went up there and I saw my horses and I killed some rabbits and I brought that meat down here for my mother and then I stayed for a week and I went back up in that hogan and I stayed up there till it was spring.

When I came down here I planted some crops and I worked on some buckskins and I wrote a letter to that Hopi and he told me when that Snake Dance is going to be and I told him I'm coming up there. I told him, "I got lots of skins and I'm coming up there for that Snake Dance."

When it was August I went up and I got two fat horses and I brought them down here and I put some shoes on them. I told my mother, "I'm going to see that Snake Dance." She said, "It's all right."

I packed my stuff on my pack horse and I started to go over there to the Hopis. I passed some Navajo camps when I was going over there but they never ask nobody to come over and stop and eat or get out of the rain. They never do that. The Hopis always give people some food but the Navajos never do. They're just like the coyotes.

When I got to Moenkopi I sold one buckskin to some Hopi for two blankets and four dollars. When I went over there to the Second Meas my friend and his wife were glad I came there. I saw that Snake Dance and I helped him in his garden and I gave him my buckskin and I got three big blankets and three saddle blankets from him. I packed them on my horse and I went over to Moenkopi and I saw that Butterfly dance again. I sure like that dance and I liked to see it.

When I was coming home it was raining all the time and all my stuff got wet. That was a heavy load for that horse and when it got wet I don't think he could carry it so I stopped and I built some fires and I dried out all those blankets and all that stuff. When the sun was shining I dried all that stuff and when it was dry again I packed it up and I went to Grand Canyon. I went over there to Rowe's Well and there was a lot of Supai boys there and they asked me, "Why do you go to that Snake Dance?" I said, "I don't like to stay in one place and just lay around. I'm going to go and see some things. When I'm dead then I'll just lay around but when I'm not dead I want to go around and see some things." Some of those boys said maybe they'll go over there and see that Snake Dance sometime.

I came down here when it was the next day. My mother dried a lot of peaches and I took them up to that storehouse on the cliff and I put them in there. We sure had a lot of peaches.

Dean Sinyella was carrying the mail down here from Grand Canyon and when it was October in that year he told me I should help him carry that mail. We carried it from down here up to Topacoba Hilltop and then we took it in a truck up there to Grand Canyon. He told me we'd stay there one night and then bring the mail back down here. He told me I could get forty dollars every month, so I told him, "I think I'll do that. I don't want to stay around down here all the time."

I helped carry that mail all winter and when it was December there was a lot of snow and we got stuck with that truck sometimes. Dean Sinyella had a camp in a cave two miles from Topacoba Hilltop and sometimes we stayed there when it was snowing hard and it was cold.

One day we got stuck bad and those chains on the wheels broke and we sure got stuck. We were stuck by a place where an old lady lived in a homestead and we could see the lights in her windows. Louis Sinyella was with me that time and it was near nighttime and we were cold. We just left that truck where it was stuck and we went over to that place and we knocked on her door. When that white lady opened the door, we could see a big heat stove and it was warm and she told us to come in there and get warm. We took our shoes off and she gave us some blankets and we wrapped up in those blankets and then she cooked some eggs and some meat and she gave us a lot to eat. She fixed a bed for us near that stove and she gave us a lot of blankets. She sure was a good old lady.

When it was the next morning she cooked a big breakfast and we sure had a lot of stuff to eat. Both of us had four eggs and a lot of bacon. She gave us some old chains and we put them on those wheels and we got out of there. That old lady was called Mrs. Lazone. She sure was a good old lady.

We had to stop lots of times before we got to Topacoba Hilltop so we could shovel out that truck. We just kept getting stuck. We had to do that all day and all night and we didn't get to Hilltop till the next day. When we got to where Dean Sinyella had a camp in that cave I froze my toes. He had a fire and we went in there and got by that fire. I had a hard time to get my shoes off because my toes were froze. When I got those shoes off I put my feet up near that fire to get them warm. Jesus Christ, it hurt me so I hollered and when it was the next morning my feet were all swoll up and I couldn't get my boots on and I couldn't walk very good. I wrapped up my feet in some rags and I got on my horse and they packed those horses up with that mail and I brought them down here. I was wondering when I was coming down here what I'm going to do if those packs got loose and I couldn't get off and fix them. Those packs stayed on all right and when I got down here I just laid around for four days and I couldn't walk good for more than two weeks and a lot of skin came off my feet.

I didn't carry no more mail all that winter. I didn't do nothing all the rest of that winter. I just laid around and I ate and I took a lot of sweatbaths. After a month I could ride around all right. When it was January I thought maybe I could go up there and trap some more but my mother and Susie told me not to go up there because maybe my feet will get bad again. I didn't go up to that place to trap but I trapped some of those raccoons down by the falls. They sure like those dried figs, and that's what I trapped them with. I got four of those raccoons and I gave two of those skins to my mother and I made some shoes from those other two and that's what I wore when I was sleeping to keep my feet warm.

When it was spring I put in some crops and my feet hurt some more and some more skin came off and my feet sure hurt a lot. I put in a lot of alfalfa. I used to have just beans and corn and melons, but I put lots of alfalfa in now. Everybody does that. I didn't ride around much or walk around much. I just worked on my garden.

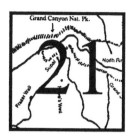

What is Dying Like?—
Mark's Mother Dies

Sometimes when it was summer I was watching those kids when they play around and swim and I was wishing I was little like that sometimes and I could play like those kids do and have some fun all the time and I wished I could have all that time for me come back again. Sometimes I'm thinking about when I'm going to die someday. Sometimes I worry about that when I hear about when somebody died. I wonder how its going to feel when I die and where am I going to live and what am I going to do. I wonder, will I work in a garden and have a house and some buckskins and stuff like I always had? Maybe I'm just going to sleep on and on. I don't think I want to do that. I was thinking about those things sometimes. I never talked about those things with anybody. I just thought about it a lot.

I worked on some more buckskins in that summer and I put some shoes on some of my horses. When I put those shoes on those horses I rode them around here to see if those shoes were all right. When I was riding around I was thinking, "Maybe I'll go up to that Snake Dance again." I told some fellows, "I'm going to see that Snake Dance" and Supai Jack said, "I always heard about that Snake Dance and I never went up there. I'm going up there this time with you." I was glad somebody was going up there with me so I don't have to go alone.

When it was the first night we camped at Rowe's Well and then the next day we went over there to Grey Mountain and there was some good feed over there for our horses. We went to Cameron Bridge the next day and we got some food there and we ate it and then we went to Moenkopi in the next day and we fed those horses there. Some Hopis there gave us some corn and some melons too and we ate some of that stuff. We went and camped maybe eight miles from there and then the next day we went to Second Mesa and we went where my friend lived. When we got there it was two days before the Snake Dance, so when it was the next day we went out and got some wood for roasting corn. We shoveled the ashes out of the hole where they roast that corn. One of the Hopi boys around there got scared and he said, "Those Snake Men are coming hunting snakes around here. If we stay around here they'll see us and they'll scare us some way. They'll get us and they'll call us a snake and they'll pull off our clothes and paint us red and make us hunt some snakes for them. If we don't hunt for snakes for them if they catch us, then we'll have to pay them a lot of stuff." We all ran away from there but one Hopi man, who used to be a Snake Man. He just stayed there and kept on working. He used to be a Snake Man and he got bit and he's not afraid of those Snake Men.

Supai Jack went to my friend's house and he just stayed in there. He sure was afraid of those Snake Men. We took off our shoes and we ran for a long way where the Snake Men don't go. We got in a wash over there and there was some shade there and we just laid down and slept all afternoon and the Snake Men didn't get us. My friend said, "We should have a girl with us when we're working around there. Then those Snake Men can't get us because they're afraid of girls. It's good to have a girl with you when those Snake Men are around."

When it was five o'clock we went back where that hole was and that Hopi man sure was sore when we left him there. When we went back to my friend's house, Supai Jack was in there and he said he sure was afraid of those Snake Men. He said he heard about a Hopi man and he was just coming near the Mesa and he had two killed sheep on his burro. He was coming from the south and that's where they hunt for those snakes on the third day. He stopped on that trail to rest and those Snake Men saw him and they ran up all around him and they all said, "Hello, snake, hello, snake." He said, "I'm a man." They told him, "Well, you're a snake." They told him they're going to put him in with those snakes and he said, "If you put me in with those snakes I'll kill all of them." They told him, "No, you can't kill those snakes. You're a partner of those snakes now." They told him, "If you don't go with those snakes you're going to pay us some stuff." He said, "All right" and he paid them those two sheep and he got a lot of stuff from the store and he gave it to them. They got fifty pounds of flour, some sugar and coffee and lots of stuff. Supai Jack said, "I'm afraid of stuff like that. I'm not going to go there where those snakes can get me." I went out to help those Hopis pick some corn, but Supai Jack, he just stayed in that house. Lots of people worked on roasting that corn and ate it all night.

When we saw that long race when it was morning, Supai Jack said, "I'm sure glad the Supais don't do nothing like that. That's too far for running." After we saw that Snake Dance, Supai Jack said, "That Snake Dance sure scared me but I'm glad I saw how those Hopis hold those snakes."

After the Snake Dance was done some Hopis told me, "In two days there's going to be a rabbit hunt all over the corn fields.

Lots of girls will be in those corn fields and they'll just stay there and make tamales and whenever you get a rabbit you can take it to one of those girls and she'll give you some tamales and you can take her in that corn and stick her all you want to." They told me, "Those girls will just give it to you if you bring a rabbit over there."

I said, "I sure want to hunt for those rabbits and get a lot of them." Supai Jack said he wanted to come back home down here. He said he saw that dance and he wanted to come home. I wanted to stay up there and stick lots of those Hopi girls. I just wanted to do that. Supai Jack said he wanted to come home. I told him, "Why don't you go home and I'll stay up here for three days?" He told me he didn't want to go home alone because he's scared of the Navajos and he wants to go before that rabbit hunt.

When it was the next day we started to come back down here and I sure was sore at Supai Jack and I didn't talk to him. We stopped at Moenkopi and then we stopped at Gray Mountain for feeding our horses. Then we went to Grand Canyon and we came home down here and I never talked to Supai Jack. Supai Jack said, "I'm sure glad we got back down here." I said, "I'm not," and I told some of those Supai boys how I missed sticking those Hope girls when Supai Jack wanted to come home. They all said, "It's too bad." Some of those boys said, "I heard those Hopi girls are good for sticking and they know how to play with you and make it so you can stick them lots of times close together"

When it was fall I went up there to Hilltop to trap some more and look after my horses. I just went up there to that hogan and that's where I stayed by myself.

Dan Hanna, my brother's son, wanted some cows and some calves and I told him, "We got no place to keep them" but he wanted to get some so I gave him three horses to take up there to those Hualapais and trade and he got two cows and two calves for those horses. When it was January, he turned those cattle loose up there on the Hualapai Trail. I didn't look after those cattle. I just let him do that. I just trapped some coyotes and some wildcats and that's all I did.

When it was March, I came down here and I planted some stuff on some of my land. The land down here was good before but now there's all Bermuda grass all over and it's hard to grow good crops. I got some of that land ready and I planted some corn and some alfalfa.

When it was April I got a letter form a Hualapai up there and he said I could work in Valentine and get some money. I went up there and I carried some bricks when they made some building up there. I worked up there till it was fall and I got a letter form down here saying Lilly Burro is sick and I should come down here and see her because I'm a relative. When I came down here she couldn't breathe good and there wasn't no medicine man down here so nobody sang for her but she got better after a week. I quit that job so I couldn't go back up there so I helped some fellows fix the trail so it won't be so hard for horses.

I took my team up there to Drift Fence when it was March and I worked on a tank. The government was paying for that tank and they fired lots of Supais when the got drunk. That sure was hard work and we got seven dollars for every day. I just worked up there in April and May and June and then that white fellow that was boss up there told us, "There isn't no more money." We all quit and after a week we all went back there and worked some more because he got some more money. We finished that work in a week and that sure was a good tank up there but no water was in it.

When we came back down here I picked some of my crops and then we had a big rain and my house was close to washed away. My mother and Susie were in there with me when all that

water came and we thought, "Maybe we'll get washed away."
Lots of people lost some crops and some stuff.

After that, me and Dan and Foster Marshall and John
Marshall went over there to Moqui Tank and we went after ten
colts from my mares over there. We went over there to get those
colts and break them to ride. Those colts sure were wild and
Dan and John said, "They're too wild to ride", so me and Foster
rode those broncs and we got them broke. Those young fellows
said those broncs were too wild but we rode them. We just kept
riding till they were broke and it was November.

Foster Marshall had a truck and one night we rode over
there to Watahomigie's place by Drift Fence and he was gone.
His wife told us, "He's gone down there to Supai and that's
where they're taking Captain Jim. He died over there in Pine
Springs.

We went back over there to Moqui Tank that night and we
were sure feeling sorry about Captain Jim. We came back down
here when it was the next day and at night they had a big funeral
for him over by Jim Crook's house and it sure was cold so we
had a big fire over there. James Wescogomie did a lot of that
singing for that funeral. He sang those Mohave songs and lots of
people danced. We danced all night and when it was the next
day they took him way up there on the Apache Trail and they
just buried him up there. They put lots of stuff in his coffin and
they put his clothes in there and some water and some food.

I stayed down here five days and then we went back up
there by Moqui tank and we kept riding those broncs and after a
while it was December and we went over there to Drift Fence to
see Watahomigie one day and he told me he heard from the
mailman that my mother is sick bad. I just came right down here
from up there and when I got down here she was near dying.
She was sick five days and I didn't hear nothing about that. She
didn't eat nothing and drink nothing and when I saw her she

didn't talk to me. Me and Henry and Susie wanted to talk to her but she didn't hear what we said. When it was near nine o'clock she was dead.

We just stayed around there and we just cried and I sure felt bad. When it was the next day me and Henry took my mother up the Hualapai Trail and we buried her up there where some of the old people were. It sure was cold and Susie and Kit Jones and Fred Hamidreek came up there too and we dug the ground and wrapped her in a blanket and we put her in there and covered her up and we put some rocks on that place and we just came away and we all cried when we were coming back here. When we got back down here we didn't go back there by Kit Jones' hogan where my mother died. We never went in there and after a while they tore that hogan down.

I was thinking about my mother and when she just worked around and when she cooked for me and when she told me lots of things when I was little. Those are things I was thinking about and that made me cry. I still think about those things sometimes and Susie does too.

I told my brother and Susie, "I'm worrying about my mother dying and I'm going away from here. I don't want to be here for a while when I'm thinking about my mother. I'm going up there to see some relatives by Peach Springs."

I went up there and I got working with those Hualapais when they were fixing that fence along the Hualapai line. I sure worked hard up there and I was glad I was working up there. I stayed in that Hualapai camp and Louis Sinyella and Martin Clinton came up there and they worked too. When it was April and May I helped fix some trails up there around the Hualapais too. Then I was thinking about going over there to the Hopis and see that Snake Dance again. I had some buckskins down here and I didn't tan them yet so I was thinking, "Maybe I'll go down there and tan those buckskins and I'll go over to the Hopis again."

I came back down here to work on those buckskins and it sure made me feel bad to come here and I cried when I was thinking about my mother. I worked on those buckskins and I got them tanned and I was working on some of those skins for my brother. I got a letter from a Hualapai they call Dave Grounds and he said I should come up there and help him dig a well and I can get some money for going to that Snake Dance. I went up there by Peach Springs and I helped him. When we were digging that well somebody shot some dynamite and a big piece of that dirt hit my head. If it was rock I would be killed but it was dirt and I was knocked over and I just laid down there and I didn't do much all day. Somebody had some pills and I took those pills and I was all right.

When it was in the middle of August I got done working up there and that Snake Dance was over so I didn't go over there to the Hopi. I came down here and then I took some horses over there west of Hualapai Hilltop and I stayed over with my horses. That place was near where a white man had a house. They called him Thornton Jones and he had some horses up there too. He had a car up there and he got some groceries for me sometimes and I didn't have to come down here for getting food. I just stayed by myself up there and Thornton Jones had to go away to a place where he lived one time and he told me to live in his house and take care of his stuff and his horses when I'm taking care of my horses too. That's what I did. I just stayed there all alone all that winter and I sure had a lot of stuff to eat, and I got lots of rabbits for meat. My brother had my gun so I just trapped those rabbits.

Nobody came around there and it just snowed all the time and I sure liked it up there. When it was spring everything was mud and I thought maybe that Thornton Jones can't come in there. When it was March he came in there all right and he brought a lot of groceries too.

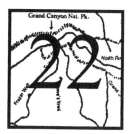

Mark Becomes a Shaman—First Time to Be Drunk

When it was April I came down here and I planted my garden. I thought about my mother all the time I was planting the garden. I kept going up on top and looking for my horses too. I only used one or two of those horses, but I liked to have a lot of them. The agent told us maybe we should sell a lot of those horses because they eat a lot of stuff and nobody does nothing with them. He said maybe we should sell those horses and get a lot of cattle but nobody has got many cattle and we like to keep those horses. We just like to have them. It makes me feel good to have a lot of horses.

I stayed down here all summer and I worked in my garden and I tanned some more hides I got from some Hualapais. When it was fall that Hualapai Doctor, Doctor Tommy, came down here. He's a relative and he said he's always a long way off and there's not enough doctors down here and sometimes they have to go out and get him if no Supai Doctors are here and he said, "There should be more doctors down here so why don't you be a doctor down here and I'll teach you." He told me he'll teach me some of his songs and it's all right for me to sing those songs if he says so. I told him, "I don't know if I can do that." We went over to where Manakadja was and he was a chief and he said, "It's all right, Mark, and you learn how to doctor." Allen Akaba was just learning some songs and Little Jim was a doctor but he was dead and Arthur Kaska was a doctor too but Doctor Tommy and Manakadja said I should be a doctor down here too.

Doctor Tommy said I should learn those songs. He gave me his rattle to sing with and he said, "Don't break this rattle or sell it or lose it or maybe my 'superstition' (spirit) will make you crazy and you'll just walk around till you fall down dead."

On that same night when it was near midnight, there was a woman who was sick and I went over there with Doctor Tommy and I listened to his songs and I learned one of them. He told me I had to learn those songs just right and then it'll be all right for me to sing them. I went over there to that place for two nights with Doctor Tommy and I learned that song. He told me, "My spirit will come to where you are when you're sleeping and you'll hear lots of songs when you're sleeping. You should sing those songs when you wake up. You sing those songs with that rattle. You keep that rattle with you all the time and you'll always have it." He told me if I sing those songs for sickness, people will get well all right.

I never dreamed none of those songs. I tried to dream songs but I never get any. Lots of times when I'm dreaming I see that spirit of Doctor Tommy and I always ask when I'm going to learn some more of those songs. That spirit just says I should wait. I wait and wait but I don't learn no more songs. I only know some songs I learned from Doctor Tommy. I never heard any from his spirit. I'm always thinking maybe someday I'll learn some more songs from that spirit. I think I will.

When I sing some of those songs when somebody's sick, those songs call that spirit of Doctor Tommy down here from the big mountain that's north west of the Hualapais. They call that place Wee-wó-qua (can see the mountain through a gap in the rocks). That's where that spirit lives and when I sing those songs that spirit comes from there to the sick man. I can see that spirit sometimes and it looks like a white bat. It's only a little one and it comes and flies around the sick man four times and then it goes in there and it pushes the sickness up near the skin and I can suck it out with my mouth. The sickness comes in my mouth and sometimes it's round and sometimes it's long; pneumonia sickness is soft and round and sometimes it's black and sometimes it's red and sometimes it's white. When I get that sickness and I put my mouth on that man where the pain hurts and that's where Doctor Tommy's spirit pushes it up where I can get it. Then I suck that sickness out in my mouth and I spit that sickness in my hand and I show it to that fellow and I tell him, "That's what makes you sick and I got it out," and then he'll get better.

I can't doctor tuberculosis or blindness. That's too hard to do and I don't know how to do it. Pneumonia is easy and I doctor pneumonia lots of times and flu and some other sickness too. I can't cure clap. That's too hard to do and I tried to cure it once but Doctor Tommy's spirit said, "It's too hard and you can't cure it."

One time Arthur Kaska tried to cure Dean Sinyella when he got that pneumonia. He couldn't cure him and I went up there and I sang for that spirit and Arthur Kaska said he didn't believe there was that spirit like a bat so I told Doctor Tommy's spirit to go over there and show him. That bat got bigger and he flew around Arthur Kaska's face four times and Arthur yelled when he saw that. Then that bat got little and went in Dean Sinyella's body and pushed that sickness up there where I could get it in my mouth and I got a lot of sickness out with my mouth. When it was the next day, Dean Sinyella got up and he just walked around and he was all right.

I doctored Thomas Yunosi and I got three long sicknesses from his arm and his leg and I showed those sicknesses to Louis Sinyella and Gilbert Marshall and Toby Uqualla and they saw them. Then I swallowed those sicknesses. Doctor Tommy told me I should swallow those sicknesses and his spirit will come and take them out of me.

All winter I just stayed down here in Supai and I cut some wood and I practiced those songs. It sure got cold down here and we had some snow. When it was cold lots of people went over there to Lemuel Paya's house and they gambled all the time and I was sure glad I don't gamble. I just cut up some skins and I made a quirt and a hackamore and I cooked for myself.

When it was spring, I put in some corn and some beans and some pumpkins. I didn't plant all my land but I had a lot of crops. I stayed down here all summer. The agent told me I should be on that Tribal Council. I didn't want to do that but he said I was on it, so I was. When we had that first meeting we talked about our boundary line. After that year I wasn't on that Council. I didn't like to do that and I don't think that Council was no good.

Some of those horses I had were old and Dan said I should sell those old horses for chicken food. I said, "It's all right." Then Dan sold those horses. He sold five of mine and four of his and he got three and a half cents for every pound of those horses.

When it was fall I picked some crops and that stuff didn't grow good. I didn't get very much stuff. Sometimes I got a lot of stuff from my crops but sometimes I don't get much. I was wondering why it's like that.

There was a Peach Dance down here in that fall and a lot of those Hualapais came down here and some Navajo boys came too. One of those Hualapais told me Thornton Jones wants me to go up there to his place again and take care of his horses when it was winter. When it was December I took my horses up there and I had six cattle too and I took them up there and I stayed at Thornton Jones' place. He called that place Buckeye and that's where I stayed.

Lemuel Paya came up there too and he brought his family too and I was glad he came up there. There was a lot of snow and it was cold all the time and Thornton Jones had a wagon up there and we hauled wood and we were warm all the time. When it was January, Thornton Jones came up here and he brought a lot of groceries and Lemuel's boy, Ralph, got two deer so we had lots of stuff to eat. Me and Lemuel tried to get some deer but we only got some rabbits. He laughed at us when we only got some rabbits but we had a lot of stuff to eat.

When it was spring, I came back down here and I put some crops in my land, but Lemuel stayed up there till it was May. Then he came down here and put some crops in too.

I always went up the Hualapai Trail every three or four days and I saw if my horses and my cattle got any water for drinking up there. If they didn't have no water I brought them down to Grapevine Spring.

When it was that spring some tourists came down here. I never packed any down here. Dan used my horses and he packed some down here but I never did that. I never talked to those tourists much. Sometimes I just said something to them when I'm riding by, but I never talked to them.

When it was June all that water got low up on top and I brought my horses and my cattle down to Grapevine Spring every three days. One of those cows had a calf, so I brought that calf down here and some of those boys used that calf to practice for the rodeo. I told those fellows, "You don't use that calf for practicing. You might kill him and then I won't have any."

When it was July I went up there to that Pow Wow in Flagstaff. I went up there with my brother, Henry. He had a car up there and I went over there with him. I took three buckskins up there but all those Navajo boys and those Hopi boys said they didn't have no money and they only had some little saddle blankets so I didn't trade those buckskins. I just brought them back down here.

When I was up there for that Pow Wow, a Hopi boy gave me a whole bottle of wine. I just drank a little of that wine and I gave it back to him, but he told me, "You keep that. It's yours." I didn't drink all that wine right away. I just drank a little sometimes. I felt like that wine was making me walk bad and I couldn't see good and I was afraid I'll get drunk and somebody will take all my stuff. I just went where we were camping and I laid in my bedding and I stayed there till it was morning. I heard my brother making some coffee when it was morning and I heard some Piute boy I worked with once come over there and he said to my brother, "Where's Mark?" My brother said, "He's over there in bed." That Piute boy came over there and he came in my bed. I turned over and I put my arms around him and then I opened my eyes and I said, "Oh, I thought it was a lady." Then we all laughed and he said, "Do you want some whiskey?" I told him, "Sure, I'll have some of that whiskey." He had a bottle in his pants and my brother came over there too and we sat in my bed and we drank whiskey. Then I went over to where those Piutes were camped. I went over there with that Piute boy and they had three gallons of wine over there and I had some of that wine. I didn't drink it so I'll get sick or get drunk. I just drank some so I'll feel good when I'm walking around.

I went over to that rodeo and I watched those boys in the rodeo and went around where they sell all that stuff and I got lots of stuff to eat and I watched all those people when they just walk around.

Lots of Supai boys got drunk and they're always fighting. I always heard the Supais get fights when they're in Flagstaff and I saw them doing that there. Some of those Navajos got in fights too and some of those boys got killed up there and I sure was glad when we came back down here. I was glad I saw that Pow Wow and I was glad when we came back down here. I don't think I want to go there again.

There was a lot of rain when we came back here and there was some flood and some dried peaches got spoiled and Mack Putesoy got fifteen sacks of corn spoiled. There was plenty of water for those horses up on the top and I didn't have to go up there and see them.

One day it was raining and I went out and I picked some corn and some beans and I got wet bad and when it was the next day I was sick and I couldn't breathe good and I had some flu. I was living in my house alone and I couldn't get some wood and some food and I sure got cold and I was sick bad. Supai Jack came over there and he saw I was sick and he took me over there to his place and the agent gave me some medicine and I got better after two weeks and I came back over here to my house and it was December.

Dudley Manakadja came over there and he said, "You got nobody to cook your food. You come over at my camp and stay over there for a while." I went over there and I just stayed there because there was somebody for cooking my food and it was warm over there and I wasn't strong yet from when I was sick.

When it was February I felt good and I went back over here to my house and I just stayed here and Dudley Manakadja came over here sometimes and he saw if I had some wood and some stuff to eat. I only had some cornmeal for eating, but I had a lot of that stuff and I had enough to eat. I made cornmeal bread sometimes too. Dudley Manakadja just came around to see if I was sick and if I was all right. He wasn't a relative. He was my friend and that's why he was looking after me. Sometimes friends are better than relatives. Relatives have to help you, friends just want to.

When it was April I put some crops in. Every year it's the same like that. West Sinyella got sick in his throat then and when he talked nobody could hardly hear him. I asked him, "Do you want me to sing for you?", and he told me, "No, I'm not sick and I'm going to be better in a few days." I said, "If you don't want me to sing for you, maybe you can go up there to that hospital in Kingman and maybe you'll get better." He told me he's all right and he don't want to go up there no place. Melvin Sinyella told him I should sing for him but he just said he's going to get better.

When it was July I didn't go up there to that Flagstaff rodeo. I didn't want to go up there and I had horses to look after too and some crops to look after. West Sinyella went up there but he was still sick.

Third Wife Comes and Goes—Work at Japanese Internment Camp

I n the next month I got a letter down here from Kate Crozier
up there with those Hualapais and he was blind and he said I
should go up there and round up some cattle he's got so he can
sell them. When it was September I went up there and I helped
him get those cattle. There was a Piute boy up there helping him
too and one day he got two horses roped together and I was
walking along and those horses ran by me on both side of me and
the rope hit me and tipped me over and I landed on top of my
head. Two boys picked me up and I was fighting with them
because I didn't know nothing for a while. They took me where
it was in the shade and they just held me down and then I started
to know something and I was all right. I was bleeding in my
head and they took me to that hospital in Valentine in a car. I
couldn't move my neck and turn my head and when we got to
that hospital, that white woman there said there wasn't no room
and she said I should go over to that Hualapai camp by Valentine
and She'll come over there and fix my head. She didn't come

over there till it was the next day and then she fixed my head. I stayed over there at Frank Beecher's camp and his wife put some hot stones around my neck so I could turn it better.

After a while I got better and I worked some more for Kate Crozier and when it was November I got through and he told me I can get that money from him when it's Christmas. I came back down here and then when it was Christmas I went back up there at Peach springs and I got that money and I just stayed up there at Kate Crozier's place all winter and I cut wood and did some stuff and that's where I stayed.

When the snow was gone and it was spring, I came back down here and I put some crops in and Supai Jack's wife was sick in her throat like West Sinyella and I sang for her. West Sinyella was still sick but he always said he's not sick.

When it was April there was some flowers on all those peach trees and then it got cold again and there was some snow down here and no fruit came on any trees that year. We only had some figs.

In that summer I got another letter from Kate Crozier and he wanted me to go up there again and help him. I told him I'll go up there after the Peach Dance so that's what I did. Kate Crozier's son was down here for that Peach Dance and I went back up there with him.

Some of those Hualapai boys helped up there too but they don't do much. Some of those boys just make themselves look like cowboys and sing like cowboys. Some of these Supai boys do that too.

I heard there was a Hualapai girl who died. She was Arthur Kaska's wife and they had her up there by Peach Springs and we all went over there and they sang a funeral. When I was over there that Hualapai girl, Eleanora Mapatis, came around me and she said, "We can get married all right." I told her, "I'll get done working with these cattle and I'll see about that." She was already married five times and I didn't like her much but I just said, "Maybe I'll do that." I saw Flyn Watahomigie by one of those camps and I told him, "I got a good wife now," and he said, "That's all right. Has she got any cattle?" I told him, "Her father's got a lot of cattle," and he said, "That's your cattle now," and then we all laughed. I wasn't married yet but I just told him that and we all laughed.

When we went out there with those cattle again it just rained all the time and there was water all over. The water was way up in that tent I was sleeping in and I had to sleep in that water. It took a long time to dry out all that stuff when the sun came out. When we got done up there I went back over there by Peach Springs to get some money from Kate Crozier and he told me he can't get some money to pay me till it's November and I just stayed there. One night Eleanora came over there and she said we should get married and I said, "No, some fellows said you're an ugly girl and you fight all the time," and she said, "No, I don't do that no more." So I said, "All right, I'll see how it's going to be." She didn't go away. She just stayed there and she came in my bed and I was married with her.

I had to wait for that money from Kate Crozier so I just stayed up there and I worked on a place where they were making a road and I carried some rocks all day. Eleanora's father worked over there too and he knew she got married with me and he said, "It's all right."

When it was December Kate Crozier got that money and he paid me and we went over there to Frazer Wells to come home down here. When we were over there a Hualapai told us, "There is a war now." He told us about that war and when it was night they told us we can't have no lights on because they might see it from the war and that'll be bad.

It snowed up there for four days and then I heard there was a fence to build over by Pine Springs and the government was paying the money so I went over there and that fence was going to be ten miles along. There was Navajos and Piutes working over there too. I just stayed with Eleanora's father and he was working on that road too. I just dug post holes and we finished that fence in three weeks and then I worked on that road again. I just stayed there and worked till it was June and then I heard about they're paying lots of money to work down near Parker and they're building a big place for those Japanese to live. Eleanora wanted me to go down there and she told her uncle he should take us down there in a car and he did. She didn't tell me about that till he was taking us down there. On the next day after we got there I got a job down there and I just cut brush for a month. It sure was hot down there and we just sweat all the time and we lived in a tent. There was lots of Navajos and Mohaves working down there too.

After a while I quit cutting brush and I sure was glad. I was afraid of all those snakes when I was cutting brush. I worked for a carpenter down there after that and then a lot of those Japanese men came there and they had some men watching them. Those guards had uniforms on and they had guns and I was kind of scared about all that. That white man I was working with, he told me to watch those Japanese and don't let them get by me and hit me on the head. One night two of those fellows with uniforms got beat up bad and they were killed I think and then they took them to the hospital and they got alive again.

I heard some white man tell all those Japanese if they don't tell who beat up those men he's going to get a whole lot of soldiers in there and kill all those Japanese. Somebody told me they got five of those Japanese who beat up those white fellows and they tied them up and they killed them. They just killed them with guns. I didn't see those Japanese get killed but that white man I worked for told me they did that. I heard they're killing some of those Japanese every week and I didn't like to stay there. Four of those Japanese got out of there and they burned up a bridge and a train fell in the river and some airplanes were all around there so they could see those Japanese and after a while they found those fellows and they took them away someplace. I don't know where they took them. I guess they killed them someplace.

I didn't like to work down there no more and I was thinking maybe they'll kill some of these Indians too and I thought maybe I'll get killed down there so I told those fellows, 'I'm going to quit." I told them, "I don't want to get killed." After that I worked for a fellow in Parker and I got five dollars for a day from him. I just piled wood where he was cutting it. When I was there I got some papers from Flagstaff about the war and I had to sign those papers. I don't know nothing about what they were. I just signed those papers and I sure was scared about that.

I just kept working down there in Parker and after a while it was June and I was rich. I had sixteen hundred dollars. Eleanora said she wanted to come back down here in Supai and pick some apricots so I just quit working down there in Parker and I sent a letter to Dan down here to come to Ash Fork in my brother's car and get us to bring us to Hilltop. We went on a train up to ash Fork and Dan didn't come there. There was a white man over there with a car and I bought that car from him. I gave him one hundred and twenty-five dollars for that car. My brother Henry showed me how to drive a car once and I drove that car home. When I was driving I couldn't keep awake and Eleanora kept hitting me. We stopped at Howard Springs and that's where we camped till it was the next day and we went to Hilltop. Nobody was up there with some horses so we walked down. We walked down to Grapevine Spring and we heard somebody coming with some horses and it was Dan and we rode down.

We stayed down here for two months and then we went up there to Peach Springs because Eleanora wanted to see her father and we only stayed up there a few days and she wanted to come back down here and dry some peaches and we stayed here till it was Christmas and Eleanora was ugly all the time. She sure was an ugly girl and I wished sometimes I wasn't married with her.

After it was Christmas we went up there to Peach Springs again and we stayed up there at that Hualapai camp and I got sick with some flu again. When I was sick Eleanora went off to Kingman and she just left me there when I was sick so I told some of those Hualapais, "She's no good to run off and leave me when I'm sick and she can't come back here with me. I don't want to be married with her."

When I got better somebody told me I can work over there in Nelson but when I went over there I got sick some more and I just quit and I went to Grand Canyon and Dan was there and I just stayed over there with him. When I got better I worked for a Mormon up there and I cut wood for him till it was summer. When it was June I heard about some working over there on the North rim. They said we can work over there and clean up some rocks on the road, so I went over there. I never was over there before and it was cold in the morning and I sure didn't like it over there. It was too cold and it was June. I quit working over there and I went around there to the South Rim in a truck and I told that mailman I wanted to come home down here but he went without me. I sure wanted to come home down here. I just walked. I walked all the night too and I guess it's maybe fifty miles to get down here and when I got down here my feet were sore and I sure was sick in my stomach. My feet were all sore and they swelled up so the teacher down here took me up to that hospital at Valentine and I stayed there three weeks and my feet got better. When I got out of that place I just went and stayed with a Hualapai. They called him Arthur Walker and he had some buckskins and he wanted me to tan them so I stayed up there and I worked on those buckskins.

When I was over there I heard one of those Hualapai boys got killed by the war and they brought him to Peach Springs. They had a funeral for him and everybody went over there. Some Hualapai boys who were in the war came over there and they had uniforms on and they made a parade for that boy. I never saw a parade for somebody who died before that, but that's what they did. They did it different because he was in the war.

When it was night Louis Sinyella sang a funeral for him and so did a Hualapai, Dick Grover. When it was the next day there was a big white man's funeral for soldiers over at Kingman and everybody went down there and that's where they took that dead Hualapai boy and he had a white man's funeral and they buried him in that white man's cemetery and there was a lot of soldiers buried there. Some soldiers shot off their guns when they were buried and some people were worrying about that and everybody cried. I don't know who covered up those graves. We just went back there to Peach Springs and somebody else covered up that Hualapai's grave. I don't think that was a good thing to do.

After four days I came home down here and my feet still hurt so I made some sweat baths and they got better. Then I went up to Hualapai Hilltop and I stayed in that cabin by the drift fence when it was fall. I had to come down here sometimes and get some food from the mail and we always had to have some papers for meat and sugar.

I had some horses up by that cabin and I just looked after them. It was cold up there but I had a lot of wood. I hunted some rabbits for meat and I was wishing I could trap some coyotes but somebody broke in that cabin and stole all my traps so I couldn't trap those coyotes. Maybe some Hualapais did that.

When it was Christmas the teacher down here asked me to cut a Christmas tree and bring it down here so that's what I did, and there was some Christmas down here and I got some socks and some cigarettes. That's all I got. I just stayed up there in that cabin all winter and when I was up there I was thinking about planting a big crop when it is spring. I was thinking about my mother and how she always had a big garden and worked hard.

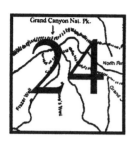

The Years Take Their Toll

When it was April I came down here and I planted a big crop like I was thinking about. I plowed up a lot of Bermuda grass and I used that harrow from the agency.

Eleanora got married with Arthur Kaska and when she was down there I never talked to her if I saw her. When it was May those Hualapais had a Pow Wow up there in Peach Springs and they took a big truck up there to Hualapai Hilltop so some Supais could go to that Pow Wow. I went and they had a circle dance up there and I sang sometimes for that circle dance.

When it was over they brought us back to Hualapai Hilltop in that truck and Arthur Kaska was in that truck with Eleanora and he was sore because I was in that truck too and he kept saying, "Maybe you're going away and marry Mark again and he'll be your husband." He just kept saying that to her and she told him to quit talking but he just kept doing that. When we got down here they were fighting all night and everybody was laughing about that. Arthur Kaska was jealous with her just like she was jealous with me. Even if I put on a clean shirt, she told me I was going out after the girls. She always said that.

Some of those Supai boys said maybe they'll have a rodeo down here when it was fall and they told me I could get some pay if I let them use my cattle for that rodeo so I said, "It's all right." They used those cattle and they had that rodeo and there was a Peach Dance, but I never got that money. I asked those fellows for that money but I never got it. After that I didn't ask them no more. I didn't say nothing and I knew I wouldn't get no money if I did say something so I didn't say nothing.

When it was October I stayed up there in that cabin and I got some more traps and I trapped some coyotes. I used some of that bait I buried up there by that hogan. It sure was strong. I took a lot of corn up there with me and some dried peaches and I hunted for a lot of rabbits and that's what I ate.

One time in that winter that Supai boy, Hardy Jones, came up there and he rode up there to my cabin and he said, "Did you see my horses?" I told him, "I don't look after your horses. Why don't you stay up on top here where you can look after yours horses?" He said, "I'll come back up here and bring my bed and I'll stay with you." I told him, "You won't come away from down there where all those girls are. You just want to lay around with those girls." He said, "Why don't you come back down there?" I told him, "I'm up here in an open place and I can look around and that's like the place I like to be when it's winter." He went away and I was thinking he won't come back. All those young boys now want everything easy and they just lay around and think they're cowboys and play with those girls. I was worrying about that and I was wondering how those young boys are going to live. Hardy Jones didn't come back up there.

One day when it was getting near night I was coming back to that cabin and I saw some smoke coming out of that chimney and I was wondering who was in that place. When I went in there I saw it was Lemuel Paya and I was glad he was up there. He said he just came up there to see if I was all right and when he was going away he said, "You be all right when you're staying up here and don't be lonesome." I said, "I don't get lonesome. I just keep going on and I don't get lonesome."

When it was April I came down here and I brought a lot of rabbit fur for Susie so she can make a blanket. Then I put some crops in my land. My nephew Dan helped me do that work. One day I told Dan, "You're a young boy now and I'm getting old now so you can have my cattle with me and we'll both own those cattle and then you'll have them all someday." He said, "It's all right." Then when it was May we sold some of those cattle and Dan got half that money.

When it was July everybody went up there to that Flagstaff Pow Wow and I didn't go. I only went up there by Hualapai Hilltop and I thought maybe I could kill an antelope and have that meat. I had a hard time to get an antelope and have that meat. I just chased them away. I was just going to quit when I saw a big buck and I just shot him for the fun but I hit him right in his heart. I sure was glad about that and I brought it down here after I skinned him and I sure had a lot of meat. I just hid that meat and nobody saw it when I brought it down here. I saw Spoonhead working in his field when I was coming home from my garden to eat at noontime and I said, "Why don't you come and eat with me? I don't want to eat alone." He said, "All right, I'll eat with you." He came to my house with me and when I got out some of that meat he just laughed and he said, "Oh, Oh! I sure want some of that meat bad." He said, "Where did you get that meat?" I said, "I grew it in my garden." He laughed and we ate a lot of that meat.

When it was the next day he came over to my field when I was working there and he said, "Let's go eat some more meat."

I said, "All right" and we ate some.

There was a lot of peaches that year and I helped Susie put away a lot of dried peaches and then I went up to Topacoba Hilltop and I just stayed up there with Foster Marshall in that winter when they went to Grand Canyon to get that mail. When it was April I went over there to Grand Canyon and I stayed over there where my brother was living. He was working up there and I stayed up there with him for a week and then I heard I can work at the Indian Camp by there where they're putting up a mission place. They called that place Jenkins Hall and I went over there and I worked on that place when they were building it.

When it was June I came back down here and I was sorry I didn't come down here before and plant some crops but I just helped Dan with his crops. When that corn was ripe I helped Dan pick it and we got lots of peaches too.

When it was winter I went up there to Grand Canyon and I stayed with my brother. I wanted to stay up there all winter but I couldn't get no job up there. I think if I was young I could get a job up there. They don't think old men can work. Some of the old Supais can work better than the young boys. The young boys are lazy. I told my brother, "I'll chop wood up here and you won't have to do that." That's what I did so I can stay up there at Grand Canyon. After a while we heard that Hualapai, Samson, died over there in Peach Springs and we all went over there and there was a big funeral. We went over there in my brother's car and that car broke down over there but some Hualapai boys fixed it up and Henry went back to grand Canyon but I just stayed over there with that Hualapai, Tom Lane, and that's where I stayed all winter. Kate Crozier brought some deer hides over there and I tanned them for him and he paid me some money and that's how I got some money.

When it was spring and the mud wasn't too deep I came home down here. Dan got a job up there in Grand Canyon and I put all those crops in by myself and looked after those horses. In that summer that white man, Thornton Jones, asked me to come up there to his place and cut some posts. I went up there and cut those posts and he let me keep my horses around there and they could drink from that cement tank he had up there. After I got done cutting these posts he asked me if I can stay up there all winter and look after his horses and I told him, "I'll do that." Then I came down here and I helped with the crops and then when it was October, I went back up there to Thornton Jones' place and it just rained all the time so there was lots of water for those horses. Lemuel Paya stayed up there too and he had his family up there. We tried to hunt for some deer but we didn't see none. I got cold sometimes when I was wet and one night after we were looking for some deer I went back to that house and I couldn't breathe good so I just laid in my bed and I got hot all over and I sure was sick and when it was the next day I couldn't eat nothing and I told Lemuel, "I sure am sick and I guess maybe I'm going to die in a few days." That's what I told him and he got a lot of wood and made that fire hot and I just laid there and Lemuel sent one of those Hualapais to take me to that hospital at Kingman and they said I got pneumonia and I was hot up to one hundred and five and I sure was sick. They put lots of those needles in me and lots of those Hualapais and my brother and some Supais came up there to see me and I sure was glad they came up there. I stayed in that place for a long time and I sure was glad I was there. If I stayed in that house I would die but I got cured in that hospital. When I went out of there I just stayed with those Hualapais at Peach Springs till it was near March and then I went to Grand Canyon on a bus and I rode in that truck with Foster Marshall to Topacoba Hilltop and then I walked down here. When I got down here I couldn't find Susie in this house and she locked it so I went to Mack Putesoy's place and they gave me some coffee and then I went back over here and Susie was here and she said, "I heard about you when you're sick. I'm glad you're all right."

I sure was tired from walking and I just laid down for two days and then I went up there to Thornton Jones' place and I didn't have no horse down here and I didn't want to ask nobody for a horse so I just walked up there. I took a short way and it was only thirteen miles. I rested two times and once I built a fire to melt some of that snow so I can have a drink of water.

When I got up there I just laid in my bedding and I was too tired. The next day I made a sweat bath and I sure felt better after that. I was glad I was still alive. When it was May I sure felt better and I just rode all around and I found all my cows and calves and they were all right and then I came home. I helped Dan put some crops in and I didn't walk around and ride much when I'm through working in the garden. I just got tired too quick. I made a lot of sweat baths and I felt better. I just stayed down here all summer. When the peaches got ripe we picked a lot and Susie dried them and I got a lot of corn too.

I wanted to go to that Snake Dance but I didn't feel like I was strong to go and I was afraid maybe it'll get cold when I'm going over there so I just stayed here. I didn't go up there to that cabin when it was winter because there was too much snow. There was lots of wood up there but there was too much snow. Lots of people got some flu down here when it was winter and the missionary gave them some medicine and they got better. Lots of people got that flu but I didn't get it. I sure was afraid I'll get sick again and I think I'll die if I get sick bad again because I'm kind of old now.

I stayed down here alone because Susie stayed up there at Grand Canyon with my brother. I just stayed here alone and I cut wood and I kept warm in my house.

When it was spring, it rained every day for almost all March and all the peach trees got flowers on them and lots of green stuff was coming up and it looked good. Dan helped me put my crops in and when it was April we had it done. When it was summer it was hot and these Supai boys were thinking about having a rodeo when it was the end of the summer and I was thinking about that rodeo too. I got a letter from the son of my friend up there with the Hopis and he asked me to come up there to that Snake Dance. He said, "Don't stay down there and see that rodeo. You come up here and see the Snake Dance." I told him, I'll come up there so when it was August I went up there to Grand Canyon and my sister, Susie, said she wants to go see that Snake Dance and have lots of that stuff to eat. Henry's boy, Alfred, took us over there to those Hopis in my brother's car. That Hualapai boy, Larry Cook, went up there with us too and we all went over there to the Hopis. We got over there in one day and I told those Hopi boys how I used to go four days to get over there to those Hopis with a horse. They laughed and we sure were glad we had that car.

That Hopi had a store over there and that's where we went and he was glad I came up there because I was his father's friend. I told that Hopi boy who are all those people I had with me and everybody shook their hands and laughed and we ate. I only had one buckskin but I gave it to that Hopi boy's wife and she sure was glad she had it and she wrapped it around her and she walked around and we all laughed and we were glad we were up there.

After that Snake Dance, Susie and those boys went back down here but I stayed up there and I helped that Hopi boy in his store and I helped him herd his sheep too. When I was there his wife's mother was sick down there in Phoenix and they had to go down there and they stayed a long time and I kept that store and I looked after his sheep. I sure liked to be in that store but I don't like looking after those sheep. They stayed down there in Phoenix for near a year and I came home after that Snake Dance.

I went up there to Desert View near Grand Canyon and I visited my brother up there before I came down here and he wanted me to stay up there and I only stayed till it was October. That was last year. I wanted to stay up there in that cabin by Hualapai Hilltop but it was too cold so I just stayed down here all winter. Dan got some deer up there and he gave me some meat and I sure had a lot of meat and I had lots of groceries too and my house was warm.

When it was the New Year everybody made a lot of noise down here and they shot off some guns. I only had one bullet for my gun so I put it in there and I went out and shot it and I heard it coming back from those cliffs like I used to hear that hollering when I was a little boy. Then I went back in my house because it was cold.

When it was April I helped Dan put those crops in but the crops weren't good this year. The land used to be good but now it's not good no more. That Bermuda grass has strong roots and it kills those crops. There didn't used to be Bermuda grass down here but now it's all over here and there's no way we can kill it. We tried to kill it but we can't do it. It's too hard and the land isn't good now.

The crops weren't good this year and we didn't get a lot of stuff like we used to. Now it's going to be winter pretty soon and it'll be cold again.

Epilogue

It was clear that in 1953 Mark, at 71, was beginning to feel his age. He was still an active man capable of a hard day's work but more deliberately and with caution. Mark died November 1, 1964 at the age of 82. His sister Susie predeceased him in 1957, nearly 100 years old. According to a number of informants, including the widow of his nephew Dan Hanna, Mark spent much of his life in those remaining years alone, wandering the rim country where "the old folks need to go", odd-jobbing here and there in places from his younger days. He never married again. He regularly came back to the canyon each spring to plant a garden and periodically through the season to tend it. He always kept a string of horses just because it made him feel good and a bit more secure to do so. He became increasingly disturbed by the inundation of the canyon by tourists and resented their intrusion into his home and his life. This seems to be one of the principle reasons he stayed out of the canyon. He had liked some white people in his life but he didn't like them in large numbers tramping through his home.

Mark made several more visits to the Hopis of Second Mesa and apparently spent one entire winter there with his friends. He continued to have periodic trouble with pneumonia and lung congestion and was finally diagnosed as having lung cancer. Sometime in the mid-nineteen seventies, he went to live with and was cared for by the Wilder family, Hualapais who lived near Peach Springs. When his condition worsened he was taken to the Phoenix Indian Hospital where he died. The Wilders took his body back to Peach Springs where he was buried somewhere on the east side of that town. His grave is not marked.

Mark Hanna. One man, one life in a time, in a place, in a culture. Insignificant among the billions of human lives but immensely important too, because it is of such lives that the human experience is made just as it is of granules of stone that the mighty walls of Grand Canyon are made.

Richard Emerick was born in Marcellus, New York in 1926. He was raised in Syracuse, New York and attended public schools there. He served in the U.S. Navy in WW 2 and in the U.S. Marine Corps during the Korean War. After graduating from Syracuse University in 1950 with a B.A. in antrhopology, he entered the University of Pennsylvania graduate program in anthropology. Service in the Korean War interrupted his program there but he returned to earn a Master's Degree and entered the Ph.D. program. He was awarded a Ph.D. in anthropology in 1960.

While in the graduate program at Penn, Emerick did field research with the Havasupai Indians in Arizona as well as 11 months of field research with the Inuit People in the Canadian Arctic and two years of research in Micronesia. The Havasupai field work, upon which his Master's thesis was based, was under the direction of Loren Eiseley, who, at that time, was chairman of the anthropology department at the University of Pennsylvania as well as the director of Emerick's Master's degree program. It was Eiseley who first recognized the importance of Mark Hanna's personal document and told Emerick that was the most important part of his Havasupai material and constituted, "a significant contribution to the use of personal document material in anthropology and to the understanding of Havasupai culture." He, along with another of Emerick's professors, A.I. Hallowell, urged its publication. Dr. Emerick's subsequent research in pursuit of the Ph.D. and, later, the development of an anthropology program at the University of Maine and a major anthropology museum at the same institution, delayed the publication of Man of the Canyon until now.

Richard Emerick is now Professor Emeritus of Anthropology and Director Emeritus of the Hudson Museum, University of Maine. He and his wife, Marilyn, live in Orono, Maine where they raised their two daughters.

Printed at the University of Maine Print Shop

Designed by Michael Fournier